Blyton™

The Enid Blyton Dossier

by Brian Stewart and Tony Summerfield

"........and this is a secret - I'd love to write a novel.....
about children, and the jolly, happy things of life".

Enid Blyton, 1926

Design: Mike Higgs

THE ENID BLYTON DOSSIER

FIRST EDITION

ISBN 1 899441 70 0

Published by HAWK BOOKS
PO Box 30, Penryn, Cornwall TR10 9YP

Artwork and Pre-Press production by
INTERACTIVE VISION LTD.,
Silsoe, Bedfordshire, MK45 4HS.

Printed and bound in Spain.

Contents

Acknowledgements...4

Foreword...5

The Enid Blyton Story...7

The Six Bad Boys...13

Golden Oldies - The Early Work...15

Fairies and Fantasy...18

The Magazines...20

Gift-wrapped Treasures - The Short Story Books.....................23

Poems, Songs and Plays...26

Green Hedges...28

Children of Adventures - The Main Series...30

Adventures Abroad...43

Children of Adventure - The One-Off Stories...44

Back to School...46

Roll Up! Roll Up! Come to the Circus!...48

Enid and the Animals...50

Nature Books...52

Down At The Farm...54

Cartoon and other Short Story Characters...56

Noddy...64

Noddy's Bits n' Pieces...69

Stories Retold...72

School Readers...73

Bible Stories and Prayer Books...74

All Things Bright and Beautiful...76

Odds n' Ends...77

The Illustrators...78

Chronology...82

Select Bibliography...96

THANKS!

WE would like to thank Barbara Stoney for her kind co-operation. Her perceptive biography on Enid Blyton is a mine of information, and she has generously shared with us the fruits of her research.

We are grateful to Enid's two daughters, Gillian Baverstock and Imogen Smallwood, for their support and for lending family photographs.

The following have also provided valuable assistance:
Pam Ally, Peter and Sheila Blackburn, Chris Beetles, Sue Bell, Christine, Michael & Richard Bunn, Janet Cooper, Nicki and Cameron Emmanuel, Fiona Pearce, Margaret Freeman, Alastair Gibson, George Greenfield, Jessica Hendriks, Cliona Kilroy, Carole and Audrey Makeham, Victoria Marks, James Neil, Catherine Porter, Mr and Mrs S.M.Simon, Sotheby's, Jeremy, Lynn, Owen and Patch Sutton-Paler, Geoff Phillips, Howard Smith, Mik and Sheila Sparrow, Lawrence and Oliver Stewart, Robert Tyndall, Nicholas Read, Ian Wallace, Clare Warner, Norman Wright. Also from Interactive Vision: Brian and Jodi Carter, Dennis Crowley, Colin Peck, John Bentley, Nigel Cave, Stuart Jelbert and Andrew Webb.

The publisher, Patrick Hawkey has with good humour enabled the 'unmanifest' to become 'manifest', and the designer, Mike Higgs has been a delight to work with. For economic reasons this book was written to an extremely tight deadline - the sort of deadline that Enid Blyton would have taken in her stride. Such pressure has only made us appreciate her genius even more.

Foreword

FOR seventy-five years children round the world have learned to read through Enid Blyton's stories: an old woman still treasures the Famous Five books that she read after being released from a Japanese prison camp, while Hindi speaking children are studying English through the same books today.

Through their letters, Enid Blyton was aware of what her stories meant to children and of the influence that she wielded. The books have stimulated children's imaginations, comforted them when they are unhappy and interested them in the natural world around them. She was both astonished and proud that her books were so loved by children of all ages and all cultures.

Gillian Baverstock   *Imogen Smallwood*

Enid Blyton aged twenty-two. The pendant she is wearing was given to her by her father on her tenth birthday. Her first husband, Hugh Pollock, described her thus: "Imagine to yourself a slim, graceful, childish figure with a head of closely cropped hair framing a face over which smiles and mischief seem to play an endless game. A pair of merry brown eyes peep out at you...clever eyes, quick to appreciate all that is passing before them".

The Enid Blyton Story

ENID BLYTON remains a publishing phenomenon - the greatest children's writer of the 20th century. She produced an outstanding body of work, attracting child readers across a ten year age group - from toddlers to adolescents. She provided a wide range of subject matter, including fantasy, re-told classics and Bible stories, school tales, nature studies, short stories, school readers, plays, poetry, circus, fairy, animal and, of course, adventure stories.

Enid brought immeasurable joy to the lives of her readers, and was responsible for so many children's continued enjoyment of reading. She published on average fifteen books a year in a career spanning over forty years - and her followers were always left wanting more.

Her clear and incisive style allowed children to exercise their imaginations and feel part of the story. Her talent for narrative, her ability to communicate with her readers, and a 'restless' typewriter produced an avalanche of work.

The Comprehensive Bibliography of the Books of Enid Blyton, lists over 1,200 entries published, republished or in the process of being published, during her lifetime - and does not claim to be complete! In addition Enid contributed to annuals and anthologies (over 200) and school readers (over 100). She was also able to write the entire contents of nearly 1000 magazines, as well as contribute to many others. Yet she didn't even have a part-time secretary and somehow still found time to write handwritten replies to hundreds of letters received from her adoring fans.

At her peak she had over twenty regular publishers and her books averaged sales of approximately 10 million copies a year worldwide. She created a one-woman industry that fuelled income and jobs in the publishing world.

She was a remarkably shrewd woman when it came to her work, and she often sold publishers series of books rather than individual titles, and included advertising references to future and past volumes within the text.

She insisted on royalties and resisted 'advance payments' on titles, because that might tie her to a publisher. If things were not going as promised she could take the book elsewhere. She insisted she had approval of the

Newnes, 1952. Cover illustration by Bernard Richardson.

THE BIOGRAPHY
BARBARA STONEY

*The centenary edition of **Enid Blyton-The Biography** by Barbara Stoney, first published by Hodder & Stoughton in 1974.*

Norman Wright correctly described this outstanding work as "a pot of biographical gold plundered by all and sundry every time they write on Blyton". - us included!

commissioning of illustrators, and of their illustrations, and had a particular input into the design of the covers, spines and page layouts. Enid demanded wide margins, good line spacing, and clear print. She dictated the 'feel' of a series, and her perceptive aesthetic taste still allowed the individual creativity of the artist to flourish.

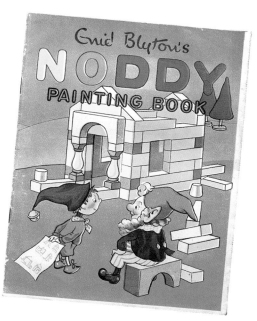

Sampson Low, 1951. The first of eleven Noddy painting books from the 1950s.

There is, nevertheless, a Blyton 'taste' to all her work. She used to say '*This is **my** book and it is going to look the way I want it to*' - and woe betide any publisher who did not conform to her wishes. The quick deterioration in the design of many reissued books after her death is a clear indication of the important role she played in the design process.

She was one of the first writers to 'logo' her name, long before many companies had come to appreciate the importance of the logo in product branding. For a woman to lead as she did in the then male-orientated world of child publishing is a testimony to strong determination and to sales-power instilled in her by young readers.

Enid Mary Blyton was born in Dulwich on 11 August 1897 in a small two-bedroom apartment above a shop at 354 Lordship Lane.

Shortly after her birth the family moved to Beckenham, where they lived first at 95 Chaffinch Road and then at 31 Clock House Road. Enid had two younger brothers, Hanly and Carey.

95 Chaffinch Road, Beckenham. Enid lived here from 1897 to 1903.

Photo courtesy of Nicholas Reed.

At Clock House Road Enid was given a small patch of garden where she delighted in growing flowers from seeds. Her father shared many of her wide range of interests and a very strong bond grew between the two. Enid would love to hear him tell stories of fairies once told to him by his Irish mother, or those based on history or the classics, and the two shared a great love of natural history, poetry and music.

She thoroughly enjoyed books and read all Arthur Mee's encyclopedias, and memorised some of the more curious facts she found there. She read a great deal of mythology and fantasy - *The Princess and the Goblin* by George Macdonald was a favourite.

She went to a small nursery school at a house called Tresco, close by. It was run by two spinster sisters and Enid seemed to be very happy there. In 1907 she became a pupil of St Christopher's School for Girls in Beckenham, and about this time the family moved to a larger house, also in Clock House Road, this time number 35.

The relationship of Enid's parents had begun to deteriorate and arguments became more frequent. Her father began an affair, and then left home for good. Enid's mother, Theresa, instructed the children to pretend to everyone their father was 'away on a visit'.

Enid was devastated. She was nearly thirteen and highly sensitive. Suddenly she not only lost her father's companionship and support, but appeared to be rejected by him too.

The fatherless family moved to a new house at 14 Elm Road, Beckenham and there Enid Blyton would lock herself away in her room for hours writing stories and poems. She immersed herself in a fantasy world that provided an escape from the pain created by her father's departure and her poor relationship with her mother.

At school Enid was expected to keep up the pretence of a harmonious family life. Not even her best friend guessed that her father had left the family. He continued to pay for piano lessons and for Enid to be

Valentine, 1944. The first storybook to use the distinctive Enid Blyton signature.

35 Clock House Road, Beckenham (left) and 31 Clock House Road (far right).

Photo courtesy of Nicholas Reed.

Enid's primary school, Tresco, at 79 Cedars Road, Beckenham (left).

Photo courtesy of Nicholas Reed.

Enid's home from 1912-1915. 14 Elm Road, Beckenham.

Photo courtesy of Nicholas Reed.

educated at St Christopher's - a private school.

There she was a great success, becoming head girl, tennis champion, captain of the lacrosse team, and winning numerous prizes for academic subjects. In her spare time she created a magazine entitled *Dab*, named after the surnames of its three contributors Mirabel Davis, Mary Attenborough and of course Enid Blyton.

Although Enid's father believed she would make her career in music, and encouraged her in this direction, her real love was for creating and writing stories and poems. She sent off examples of her work to numerous magazines, and received countless rejections.

In the summer of 1916 she stayed with friends of Mabel Attenborough (Mary's aunt) at Seckford Hall, near Woodbridge, Suffolk. Ida Hunt, one of the daughters of her host, took her to the Woodbridge Congregational Sunday School. There she discovered her talent as a teacher telling Bible stories. That September she enrolled on a National Froebel Union course at Ipswich High School. The start of her career saw her contact with her family virtually cease.

She still managed to find time to write, and in 1917, at the age of twenty, the first recorded publication of an Enid Blyton work appeared - It was a poem entitled 'Have You...?'. At the end of the following year she qualified as a teacher and soon took up a post at Bickley Park School, where the children loved to hear her make up stories.

From there, Enid moved to Surbiton to take up a post as a nursery governess to four children, who adored her. In her spare time she continued to write.

From 1921 her short stories and poems were featuring in *The Saturday Westminster Review*, *The Bystander*, *The Londoner* and *The Passing Show*. The following year her first book, *Child Whispers*, a collection of poems, was published by Saville. It was well received and was successful enough for them to publish four more of her books in the next two years.

Through her work for another publisher, Newnes, she met the editor, Major Hugh Pollock in 1923. They fell in love and were married in August the following year.

At first they lived in a flat in Chelsea, but Enid had begun to earn a large annual income from her writing, and together with Hugh's salary the couple were able to move in 1926, to a newly built house in Shortlands Road, Beckenham, which they named Elfin Cottage.

St Christopher's School, Beckenham. Enid is 3rd. from right in the middle row. Her friends, Mary Attenborough, Phyllis Chase and Mirabel Davis are all in the top row, 3rd., 4th., and 5th. from left respectively.

Enid Blyton in 1923.

Back of Elfin Cottage, Shortlands Road, Beckenham.   Photo courtesy of Nicholas Reed.

Old Thatch, Bourne End, Buckinghamshire.
Photo courtesy of Nicholas Reed.

In the spring of 1928, because of her difficulty in conceiving a child, she consulted a gynaecologist. His diagnosis was that Enid had an unusually undeveloped uterus 'almost that of a young girl of 12 or 13'. Enid's biographer, Barbara Stoney, considers that this was yet another indication of the far reaching effects her father's departure had on her. Enid was put on a series of hormone injections.

When 'a great new arterial road' threatened the haven of Elfin Cottage they moved, in 1929, to Old Thatch at Bourne End, Buckinghamshire close to the River Thames. With them went Bobs the dog - a fox-terrier who, with Enid's help, wrote letters in *Teachers World*, and who had a readership all of his own. In 1933 *Letters from Bobs* was published privately by Enid and within its first week it had sold 10,000 copies.

The birth of her daughter Gillian in 1931, was followed in 1935 by the birth of Imogen. Nannies, a Chaffeur-gardener, a cook-general, and a succession of housemaids ensured that Enid was able to keep up her writing. She was more

capable of expressing her love for children through the written word than she was in reality.

There were a number of sides to her complex personality, and although she possessed sophisticated adult skills in her business and writing career, emotionally she was a child, too immature and vulnerable to cope fully with motherhood. Often real motherhood was delegated to others.

In 1933, Hugh was particularly busy at work with several notable authors under his wing, including Winston Churchill, who was producing an abridged version of one of his books which covered the First World War. During their discussions, Hugh found himself reliving some of the traumatic experiences he had tried to forget and this, added to the increasing pressures of his work at Newnes, resulted in a breakdown in his health and a return to using alcohol as a temporary palliative, as he had often done on his leaves from the trenches.

This was to be the pattern over the following few years at times of stress and the situation was not helped by what he felt was his gradual exclusion from Enid's life by her successful writing and, later, by her close friendship with Imogen's maternity nurse, Dorothy Richards.

After his recovery from a severe bout of pneumonia in the late 1930s, and Enid's concern over its seriousness, the marriage went through a brighter phase, but this was to prove shortlived.

Christmas card illustrated by Phyllis Chase with verses by Enid. circa early 1920s.

Just before the outbreak of war, the family moved to a house in Penn Road, in Beaconsfield, which Enid named 'Green Hedges'. After the declaration of war, paper rationing was imposed on publishers. To cope with these restrictions she just increased the number of publishers she dealt with.

In 1940, Hugh, at the age of fifty-one, rejoined his old regiment, and was posted to Dorking, where he trained Home Guard officers. While in the process of recruiting staff to join him, he had chanced to meet one of Newnes' young novelists, Ida Crowe, working at the War Office and engaged her as his secretary. Later Hugh's work with the army was important enough for him to be placed on a Nazi priority list for extermination.

Hugh's first wife had been unfaithful to him when he was in the trenches during World War I and this added to his general insecurity over his marriage to Enid. When he heard on his first Christmas leave that she had been entertaining other men in his absence he confronted her on the

Macmillan, 1942. The first book to be illustrated by Eileen Soper and the first book to carry the familiar signature.

subject and there was a furious argument between them. The marriage never recovered and, on his return to Dorking, he sought consolation for the first time with Ida Crowe.

While on holiday with her friend, Dorothy Richards, Enid met Kenneth Darrell Waters, a surgeon. A romance soon blossomed. Enid took the lease of a London flat in Dorothy's name, and a regular rendezvous occurred. It seems that it was after Enid's affair with Kenneth, that Hugh finally gave up hope and turned to the novellist Ida Crowe, who had apparently loved him for some time.

A divorce was settled in which, for Enid's sake, Hugh agreed to be cited as the guilty party, provided he was given access to the children. After the divorce in 1942, Enid quickly married Kenneth. She did not comply with the agreement she had made with Hugh, and the poor man never saw his daughters again. Their surnames were changed by deed poll to Darrell Waters.

Enid continued to write tirelessly with astonishing success. The sales of her books made her a wealthy woman, as well as creating valuable income for publishers, agents, administrators, illustrators, printers, paper merchants, transporters and book sellers.

In 1950, she was advised to set up her own copyright assignment company, and named it Darrell Waters Limited.

*An illustration by Eileen Soper from **The Runaway Kitten**, Brockhampton, 1945. As a child Enid was not allowed to keep pets. She found a kitten and kept it secretly. When the animal was discovered she was made to give it away.*

Enid Blyton at Green Hedges.

At the back of the photograph of Enid at Green Hedges, placed on the table, is the Noddy doll given to Enid for Christmas in 1951 or 1952. (see insert).

Because of Enid's prolific energy rumours started emerging that she employed a team of writers to assist her.

In the late 1950s these rumours had become so strong that Arnold Thirlby, her lawyer, had to take legal action against a South African librarian who kept repeating it in public. This resulted in a public apology in court.

Her hard work was eventually to have an adverse effect on her health. By 1960 the first symptoms of Alzheimer's disease became evident. It very slowly took hold and at the end of her life her lucid moments became fewer and fewer. She made contact again with her brother Hanly, but when he visited her she did not recognise him. After it was established that he was indeed a brother, she wanted to return immediately to 'Mother and Father'. She could only remember the happy times before her father left.

After Kenneth died, she was looked after at home by her faithful housekeeper, Doris Cox, until a few months before her death in a nursing home in Hampstead on 28 November 1968.

The Six Bad Boys

WHILE researching her pioneering biography on Enid Blyton, Barbara Stoney made a remarkable discovery. She was drawn to Enid's book *The Six Bad Boys*, because of a chance comment in a review.

On reading the book she found to her amazement that Enid had written about the traumatic night when her father left home for good. Thinly disguising her involvement by reversing the sex of the characters, Enid placed herself as Tom. Here are some of the extracts noted by Barbara Stoney:

'She had nagged him as usual, and then one of the usual rows had flared up, all in front of the three children. The girls began to cry, and Tom stood up to go out of the room in disgust. But something his father had said made him stop.

He spoke in a quiet voice. 'This is the end. It's not good for any of us to go on like this. I am sure that you are right when you say I am to blame for everything. So I'm going. Then perhaps you will be happier, all of you.'

He left the room without another word, brushing by Tom. He went upstairs and they heard him opening drawers and cupboards. Eleanor tore upstairs too.

'Dad! What are you doing? Don't go! I don't want you to go!'

Her father said nothing, but clipped shut his big suitcase. He didn't even look at Eleanor. She shrank back from his stern white face. He looked suddenly much older.

The front door slammed. The front gate clicked shut. Quick footsteps went down the lane, and then faded away.

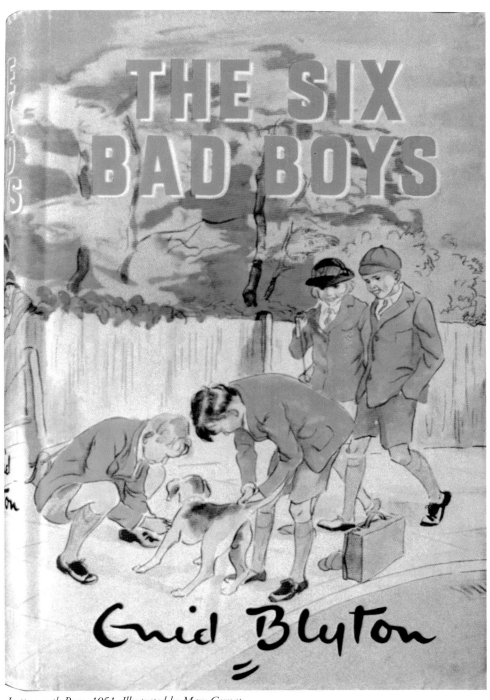

Lutterworth Press, 1951. Illustrated by Mary Gernat.

'He's gone!' wailed Hilda. 'I don't want him to go.' 'He'll come back,' said her mother, dabbing her eyes. 'He did before.'

But Mr Berkeley **didn't** come back! No one put a key in the front door that night and crept upstairs. No one slept in the bed in the little dressing-room. Mr Berkeley didn't come back!

That was a dreadful time for the three children. They had to cope with a tearful, complaining, angry mother, who had no idea where her husband was. They had to promise her not to tell anyone their father had gone away because of a row. They were to say he was on a visit. They had to face the fact that perhaps their father might never come back.........

....They missed him much more than they had ever dreamed they would. They kept asking their mother where he was, and if he was coming back.

*Enid promoting her book **The Six Bad Boys**, c.1951.*

She was very subdued one day. She had a letter, a serious letter. 'He's made up his mind not to come back,' she said. 'He's sending us money every month. Oh, why has this happened to me?'.

All three children could have told her; but they said nothing. They stood there, looking profoundly dismayed. They felt as if their home was breaking up.........

......They missed their father; they hated having to pretend he was coming back at any moment; and their mother was so harassed and felt herself to be such a martyr that there was even less peace and comfort in their home than there had been before.

When Barbara Stoney showed these passages to Enid's brother Hanly, he was obviously very moved and he

wiped a tear from his face. "Yes, that's us," he said "it is exactly what happened. I never knew she had written about it all.".

Ironically, the book was described by an unsuspecting critic as *'a rare and unsuccessful attempt at social realism'.* Reality is sometimes stranger than fiction!

Enid had loved her father deeply and was badly hurt. She felt rejected. Unable to cope with her sensitive emotional feelings, her answer was to shut out her suffering by escaping to her writing. It was so successful a defence mechanism that it became an addiction. In some respects it was easier to keep herself busy and project her love through her writing than to let that love risk rejection in the real world.

Barbara Stoney, the highly acclaimed author of **Enid Blyton-The Biography,** *at home in 1998 with her copy of* **The Six Bad Boys.**

Illustration by Mary Gernat from **The Six Bad Boys.** *Lutterworth Press, 1951.*

ENID'S first two published poems, one for *Nash's Magazine* and the other for Arthur Mee, have not been traced. Her first known poem was 'Have you.......?' in *Nash's Magazine,* March 1917.

She won a prize for her essay 'On the Popular Fallacy that to the Pure All Things are Pure' in *The Saturday Westminster Review*, February 1921. In the year that followed she was to have her first stories published. These were written for adults, with titles such as 'The Man She Trusted', 'Aunt Jerusha's Earwig', 'Vantage In' and 'The Reward of Virtue', which appeared in *Home Weekly, The Londoner, The Bystander* and *The Passing Show* respectively.

*Above: **Child Whispers**, Enid's first book, published by J.Saville & Co. in 1922. Illustrated by Enid's schoolfriend Phyllis Chase. Right: Original artwork by Phyllis for the 1923 edition.*

Enid's first book of poems, *Child Whispers*, was published by J.Saville & Co. Enid had arrived!

During the 1920s and 1930s she contributed a host of stories and poems to a whole variety of annuals for firms such as Cassell, Newnes, Nelson and Renwick. Some were published under her own name, others under the pseudonyms of Audrey Saint Lo, Christopher and Becky Kent. Her work was also being published in periodicals such as *The Morning Post, Child Education, Teacher's Times, The Schoolmistress, Punch, The Lady,* and John Leng's *Fairyland Tales.*

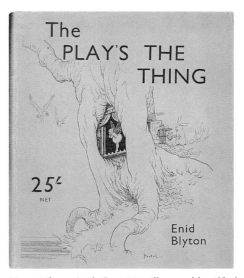

Home Library Book Co.,1927. Illustrated by Alfred E. Bestall. This book was her most expensive.

*Illustration by Harry Rountree for **Nursery Stories**, Dean, 1922. This was Enid's first story to be published in book form.*

1922 saw a change of direction, and in February her first children's story, 'Peronel and His Pot of Glue' was published in *Teachers World*. In June of that year she had her first two children's stories published by Dean in book form - 'The Adventures of Bob Bunny' in *Nursery Stories* illustrated by Harry Rountree and 'Waddles' (a tortoise not a duck!) in a book of the same title illustrated by Kathleen Nixon. In the same month

Newnes,1926. Illustrated by Roland Green.

Birn Brothers,1927. Illustrator unknown.

Birn Brothers,1927. Illustrated by K.M.Waterson.

Nelson,1928. Illustrated by I.Bennington Angrave. One of only two books written in the first person. Enid recorded the book in her diary: "My new book published by Nelson's arrived today. It's lovely, very artistic".

Back cover illustration by Molly Benatar for **Cheerio!** *published by Birn Brothers in 1933.*

Some of Enid's early writing remained anonymous, but thanks to a detailed record that she kept during this period most is traceable.

There are, however, a number of books produced by Birn Brothers still waiting to be 'discovered' (the reason why no Blyton bibliography can be called complete!). After initially producing verses for both Christmas and Birthday cards, Enid wrote a large number of cheap books for the company and as yet relatively few have come to light.

Amongst those that have is *The Wonderful Adventure* published in 1927. It is her first known full-length adventure story, and has the unusual distinction of being one of only two books that Enid wrote in the first person. The other *Let's Pretend* was published by Nelson a year later. Obviously she found this style didn't suit her.

The Green Goblin Book published by Newnes in 1935. Cover illustration by Ian Hassall with text illustrations by Gordon Robinson. Unusually this book had two dust jackets, this is the 'under' one.

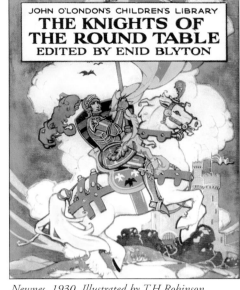

Newnes, 1930. Illustrated by T.H.Robinson.

The Book Around Europe, a novelty publication by Birn Brothers c.1929, with a rotating dial on the front.

Sports and Games published by Birn Brothers in 1924. Illustrated by Richard Ogle. One of the earliest books by Enid to contain original fiction. The book was re-published in 1932 with a new title.

Silver and Gold, published by Nelson in 1925 and illustrated by Lewis Baumer. This small book of poems sold well enough foe Nelson to produce a deluxe edition two years later illustrated by Ethel Everett (right).

My First Reading Book published by Birn Brothers in 1933. Illustrator unknown.

Birn Brothers, c.1927. Illustrator unknown.

Birn Brothers, c.1927. Illustrator unknown.

Birn Brothers, c.1929. Illustrator unknown.

Fairies and Fantasy

MUCH of Enid's earliest writing was about children's encounters with the 'little folk' and the train of her imagination made frequent stops at Fairyland.

Some wonderful titles appeared in annuals of the early 1920s - 'Kaliss, Higgletop and the Sillybillies', 'Giant Sleepyhead and the Magic Towers' and 'The Jobbernolls and the Ball of Golden Fire'. A child's attention was gripped from the opening line, as in 'Tarrydiddle Town' - 'Molly lived with her mother and father right on the edge of a magic wood'.

Enid's first collection of short stories was titled *The Enid Blyton Book of Fairies*, an annual-sized gift book from Newnes, with a wonderful colour frontis by Lola Onslow and a map of Fairyland drawn by Horace Knowles.

Other books in the same large format followed. In the 1920s there was *The Enid Blyton Book of Brownies*, and in the 1930s *The Red Pixie Book, The Green Goblin Book* and *The Yellow Fairy Book*.

It was not surprising that with the relaunch of *Sunny Stories* and the emergence of Enid's first full-length serialised stories, that she should turn first to a genre that she felt fully comfortable with and two fine fantasy series followed - The Wishing Chair and later The Faraway Tree.

The Wishing Chair

In the two Wishing Chair books Mollie and Peter have a number of fantasy adventures with Chinky the pixie. Although there was a thirteen year gap between the two books, there were two short stories published in *Sunny Stories* in between. An additional short story appeared in *Enid Blyton's Omnibus*. All the stories were illustrated by Hilda McGavin.

1. *Adventures of the Wishing Chair*, 1937
2. *The Wishing Chair Again*, 1950
plus
'The Wishing Chair Again' *Sunny Stories*, Nos. 91 & 92, October 1938
'Santa Claus and the Wishing Chair', *Sunny Stories*, Nos. 101 & 102, December 1938
'Good Old Wishing-Chair', *Enid Blyton's Omnibus*, 1952

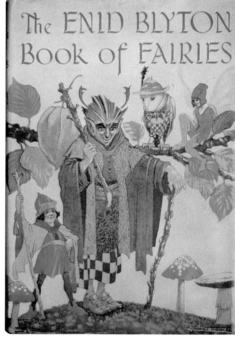

Below: Newnes, 1949. Illustrated by Horace Knowles.

The Faraway Tree

The Faraway Tree in the Enchanted Wood contains a number of strange lands where Jo, Bessie and Fanny go through a series of magical adventures. There are three books and a short story together with a picture strip book *Up the Faraway Tree* which is normally included in a series of eight picture strip books. Dorothy Wheeler's superb illustrations add to the magical atmosphere.

1. *The Enchanted Wood*, 1939
2. *The Magic Faraway Tree*, 1943
3. *The Folk of the Faraway Tree*, 1946
plus

Up the Faraway Tree, 1951
'The Faraway Tree', *Enid Blyton's Omnibus*, 1952

Left: Illustration by Eileen Soper from The Dog That Went to Fairyland, Brockhampton, 1944.

*First two editions of **Real Fairies**, published by J.Saville & Co. in 1923 and covers illustrated by Phyllis Chase. This was Enid's third book.*

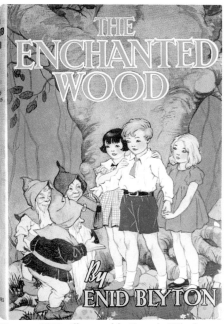

Newnes, 1939. Illustrated by Dorothy Wheeler. First in series.

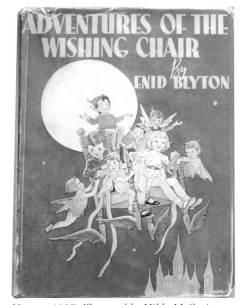

Newnes, 1937. Illustrated by Hilda McGavin. First in series.

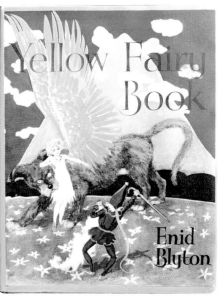

Newnes, 1936. Illustrated by H.R.Millar.

Newnes, 1943. Illustrated by Dorothy Wheeler.

Newnes, 1946. Illustrated by Dorothy Wheeler.

Newnes, 1950. Illustrated by Hilda McGavin.

Newnes, 1951. Illustrated by Dorothy Wheeler.

19

The Magazines

EARLY in 1926, Newnes decided to bring out a series of cheap, magazine-type books, and with Enid Blyton at the helm *Sunny Stories for Little Folks* was born.

The first two issues appeared in the shops in July 1926 and for the next ten years, two new titles were added each month.

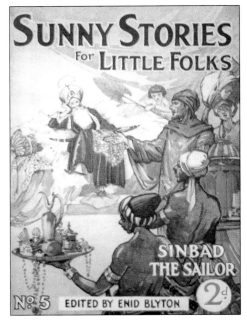

Sunny Stories for Little Folks No.5,
September 1926.
Cover illustration by Dorothy Newsome.

Although the words 'Edited by Enid Blyton' were used on the covers, she in fact wrote every story that was to appear in the 250 issues.

In the early days there was a good mix of full-length stories and short stories, some of which were original, whilst others were Enid's re-told versions of familiar favourites such as Sinbad and Gulliver.

After eighteen issues the three-coloured cover turned into full-colour and with the 'books' undated they enjoyed a long shelf life at the newsagents - with up to fifty titles being available at the same time.

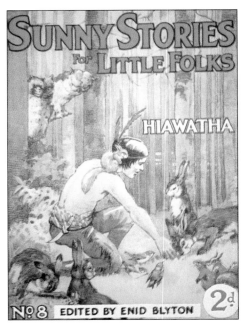

Sunny Stories for Little Folks No.8,
October 1926.
Cover illustration by Kathleen Nixon.

Sunny Stories for Little Folks No.20,
April 1927.
Cover illustration by Dorothy Newsome.

There was a change of style from number 57 onwards. The price dropped from 3d to 2d, the familiar red border was used for the first time and the contents were made up entirely of original short stories - separated by the occasional poem. For about a year or so there was also a letter from Enid, first from Elfin Cottage and later from Old Thatch.

In January 1937 there was a complete change of direction. A move from 'book' to weekly

magazine was adopted, and a new series was started with the title *Enid Blyton's Sunny Stories*. Due to a wartime paper shortage it became a fortnightly issue from number 273 and four issues later the title was changed again to become just *Sunny Stories*.

Full-length books were serialised and new characters, such as Amelia Jane, were soon to make a regular appearance.

Sunny Stories for Little Folks No.23,
June 1927.
Cover illustration by W.S.Foyster.

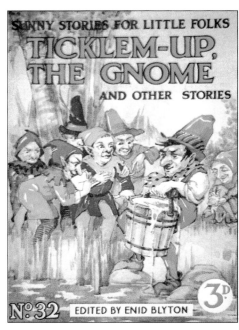

Sunny Stories for Little Folks No.32,
October 1927.
Cover illustration by Kathleen Nixon.

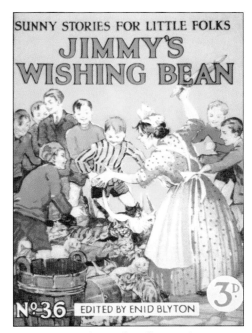

Sunny Stories for Little Folks No.36,
December 1927.
Cover illustration by Dorothy Newsome.

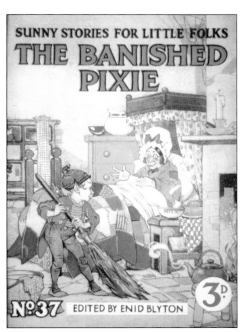

Sunny Stories for Little Folks No.37,
January 1928.
Illustrator unknown.

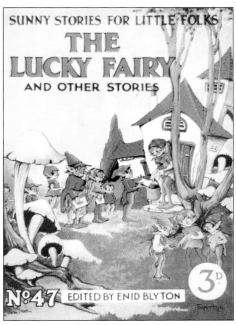

Sunny Stories for Little Folks No.47,
June 1928.
Cover illustration by Joan Hoyle.

Sunny Stories for Little Folks No.55,
October 1928.
Cover illustration by Kathleen Nixon.

Sunny Stories for Little Folks No.113,
March 1931.
Cover illustration by Sylvia Venus.

Sunny Stories for Little Folks No.118,
May 1931.
Cover illustration by Hilda McGavin.

In 1952 there were rumblings of discontent. Enid felt she had too little control over the style and content and Newnes stubbornly refused to advertise anything other than their own products. She began negotiations with Evans and with her final issue on 19 February 1953, Enid and *Sunny Stories* parted company. After a period of twenty-seven years and a total of 803 magazines, there wasn't even a farewell letter in the final issue. They had lost their 'star', but Newnes continued as if nothing had happened and several months later in her own magazine Enid told her readers most firmly that she no longer wrote anything for *Sunny Stories*.

On 18 March 1953, just a few weeks after parting company with Newnes, *Enid Blyton's Magazine* was launched. Over the next six years this was to become the vehicle for her four charitable societies and much of her merchandise was advertised in its pages.

There was also a long chatty introductory letter in each issue. Due to a paper strike in 1959, this magazine also had a somewhat abrupt ending - but this time a letter full of regret was published. The magazine had lasted 162 issues.

The contents of these two magazines, and to a lesser extent her regular contributions over a twenty-three year period to *Teachers World*, were to provide the bulk of her total output of short stories, which numbers approximately 5000. Many of these have been cleverly recycled in series of short story books from various publishers and very few new short stories were written for books. Although Enid's magazines came to an end nearly 40 years ago, the short stories, serialised books and the many characters, which first saw the light of day within their pages, live on.

Promotional leaflet to launch the new magazine.

Early trial dummies for what was to become Enid Blyton's new magazine, November 1952.
Cover illustration by Eileen Soper.

Left: **Enid Blyton's Magazine** *Vol.1, No.1, March 18th., 1953.*

Right: **Enid Blyton's Magazine Annual**, *published by Evans in 1954.*
Cover illustration by Grace Lodge.

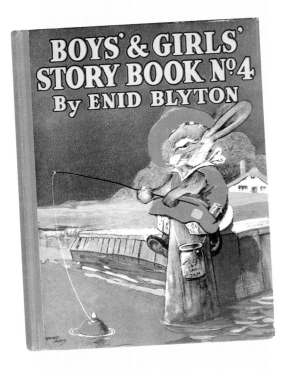

*Published by **News Chronicle**, 1936.*
Cover illustration by Ernest Aris.

WITH a deep reservoir of stories at her disposal, Enid was able to produce a wonderful range of short story books. Many of these were to form part of a long-lived series, with an eagerly awaited new book being added annually.

The first series in the 1930s, published by the News Chronicle, came as boxed editions. All that followed were 'gift-wrapped' in superb dustwrappers, illustrated by such artists as Hilda Boswell, Eileen Soper, Joyce Johnson and Grace Lodge. Series such as the Holiday Books and the Flower Books also had some magnificent colour plates and the wide variety of top artists credited for the text illustrations read like a who's who of children's illustrators.

Published by Hodder & Stoughton, 1942.
Illustrated by Eileen Soper.

*A selection of first editions of the **Holiday Books** published by Sampson Low between 1946 and 1955.*
Cover illustrations are by Hilda Boswell except for Vol.6 which is by Robert MacGillivray and Vol.9 which is by Cicely Steed.

First editions of **The Bedside Book** series published by Arthur Barker between 1949 and 1957. Cover illustrators are unknown except for Vol.1, Whyte, Vol.5 & Vol.7, Joyce Johnson and Vol.6, Grace Lodge.

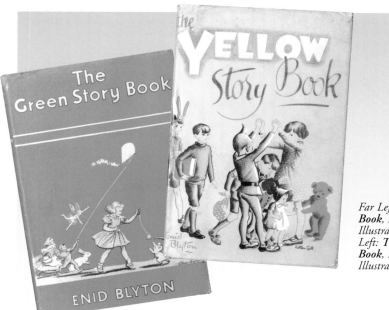

Far Left: **The Green Story Book**, Methuen, 1947. Illustrated by Eileen Soper.
Left: **The Yellow Story Book**, Methuen, 1950. Illustrated by Kathleen Gell.

Hodder & Stoughton, 1949. Illustrated by Grace Lodge.

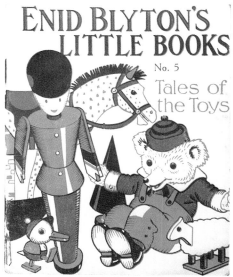

Evans, 1942. Illustrated by Alfred Kerr.

Evans, 1944. Illustrated by Nora Unwin.

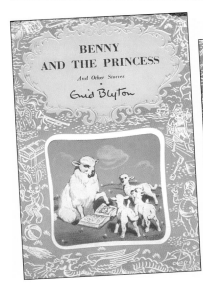
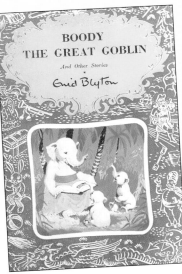

Part of a series of short story collections published by Pitkin in 1951. Cover illustrators unknown.

National Magazine Co., 1946. Illustrated by Gwen White.

Latimer House, 1952. Illustrated by Grace Lodge.

Brockhampton, 1954. Illustrated by Eileen Soper.

Harold Hill, 1948. Illustrated by Frank Varty.

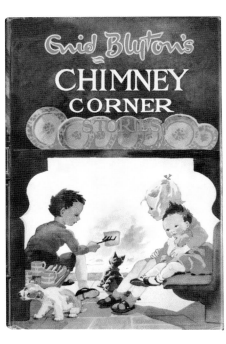

Latimer House, 1953. Illustrated by Grace Lodge.

John Gifford, 1954. Illustrated by Hilda Boswell.

Poems, Songs and Plays

ALTHOUGH Enid started her career with poetry, as the demand for narrative books increased, she wrote less and less verse. Much of her best poetry was written in her early years. *The Enid Blyton Poetry Book* of 1934, was in fact her final book of poems, and these were all collected from material previously published in *Teachers World*.

There were also over 300 poems in *Sunny Stories*, but gradually they appeared less frequently, until the final one in August 1941. She did write about twenty poems for her magazine, and there were also a few in short story books, but overall the last three decades of her career were fairly barren as far as verse was concerned.

Some of her poems were set to music using a variety of composers, with Alec Rowley emerging as a favourite. She probably published less than a dozen songbooks, the final one published in 1965, came from a collaboration with her nephew Carey Blyton, entitled *Mixed Bag*.

Her short plays were also mostly written in the early part of her career, prior to 1940. Books of plays produced after this date were merely a collection of her earlier work.

During the 1950s Enid produced three full-length plays. The first was really a pantomime revolving around Noddy, but also including other favourites such as Mary Mouse, Mr. Pink-Whistle, the three Gollies and various folk from the Faraway Tree series.

This enjoyed annual success during the Christmas period for several years, and at one time was running simultaneously in London and Manchester. It was published in a lavishly illustrated book in 1956 and filmed in 1958.

Fired by the success of Noddy, she stepped up an age group for her next play, about the Famous Five. The plot bore a strong similarity to *Five Have Plenty of Fun*, which is probably why the play was never published. It ran for two years. In 1964 it was enjoying success in Paris at the Theatre Des Enfants, with Timmy treading the boards under the name of Dagobert!

Her third and final full-length play was another step up the ladder - this time for adults and sadly it proved a rung too far. Written under the tongue-in-cheek name of Justin Geste, the initial title *Summer Storm* had changed to *Out of the Blue* on the title page.

Unfortunately, there were no takers and like her one attempt at an adult novel some twenty or so years before, it also remained unpublished and in this case unperformed.

J.Saville & Co., 1923. Illustrated by Phyllis Chase. This was Enid's second book and the only book for which she also composed the music.

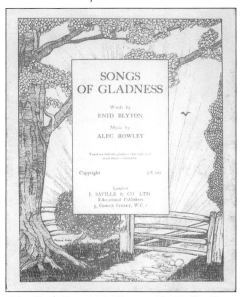

J.Saville & Co., 1924. Illustrated by Phyllis Chase.

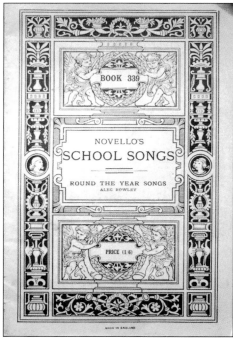

Novello, 1931.

Boosey & Hawkes, 1965.
Music by Enid's nephew, Carey Blyton.

Both books published by Newnes in 1940.
Illustrated by Alfred E.Bestall with music by Alec Rowley.

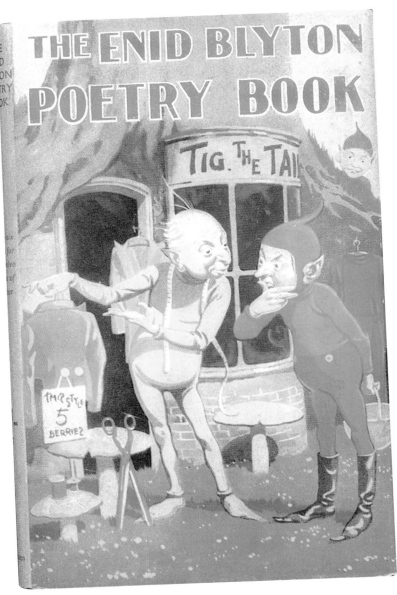

The Enid Blyton Poetry Book.
published by Methuen in 1934.
Cover illustrated by Geo.S.Dixon.

Six Enid Blyton Plays.
Published by Methuen
in 1935.
Cover illustrator
unknown.

Mr. Sly-One And The
Cats.
Published by Evans
in 1955.

"Happy Year" Song
Book.
Published by J.B.Cramer
in 1955

Green Hedges

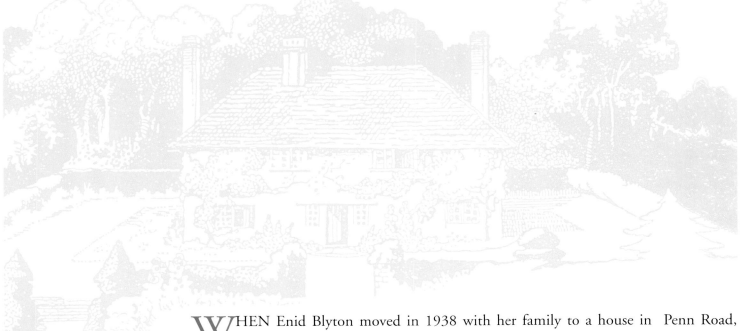

WHEN Enid Blyton moved in 1938 with her family to a house in Penn Road, Beaconsfield she asked her readers what she should call it, and by far the most popular name was Green Hedges. The seven-bedroomed house stood proudly in two-and-a-half acres of grounds, and stood well back from the tree-lined road. Enid wrote a poem to mark the move.

Green Hedges

What shall we call you, little new house,
With your chimneys red and tall?
Your leaded windows and cosy nooks,
Your sunny corners and smiling looks,
And your creepers all over the wall?

I think we shall love you, little new house,
With your big trees all around,
And your quaint green hedges and secret bowers,
Your hidden lawns and your glowing flowers,
Your daisies all over the ground!

Will you shelter us well, you little new house,
And welcome my family here,
And love my two little girls at play,
With their birds and animals happy and gay,
For many and many a year?

We'll call you Green Hedges, little new house
It's just the right name for you,
We'll be like the birds for they build their nest
In the hedgerows high that they love the best
And we'll build in Green Hedges, too.

Unfortunately, '*build in Green Hedges*' is exactly what happened. After Enid's death the property was sold by auction on 26 May 1971. Purchased by developers it was demolished in 1973 to make way for a housing development.

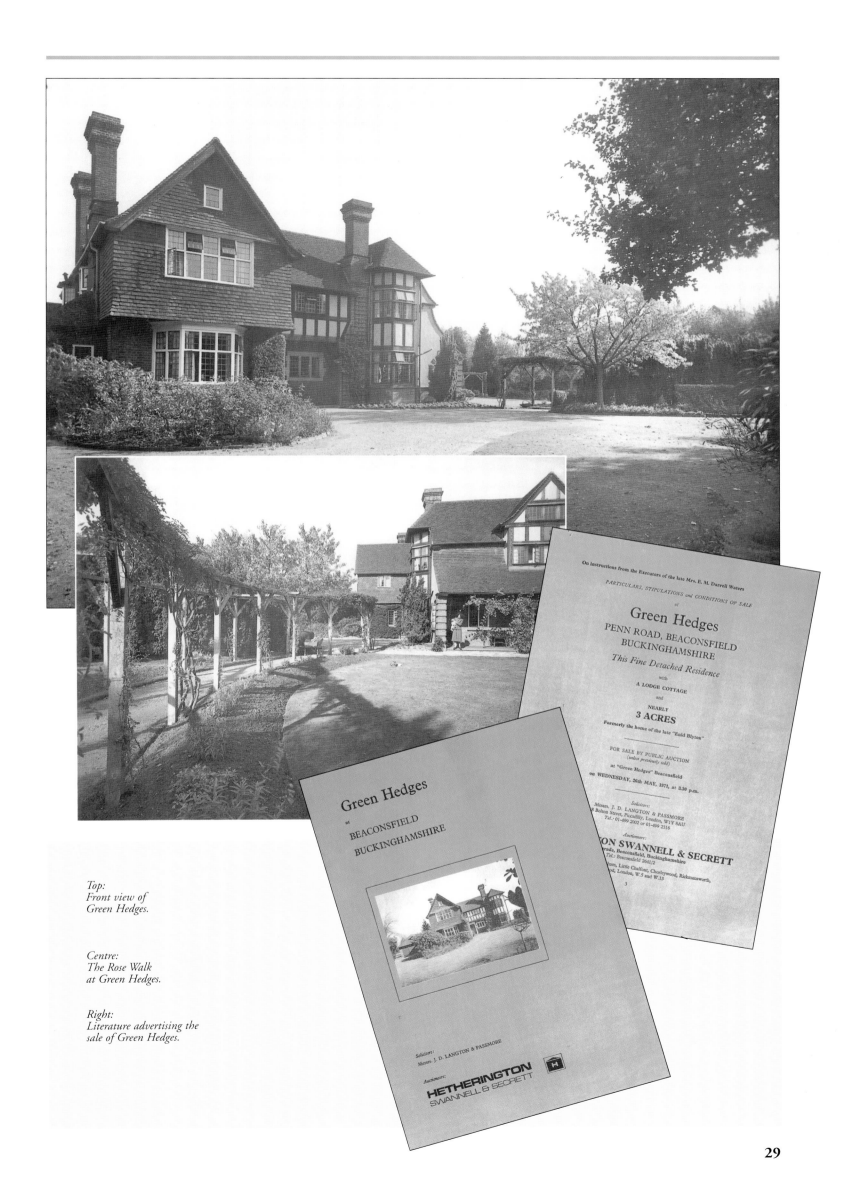

Top:
Front view of
Green Hedges.

Centre:
The Rose Walk
at Green Hedges.

Right:
Literature advertising the
sale of Green Hedges.

On instructions from the Executors of the late Mrs. E. M. Darrell Waters

PARTICULARS, STIPULATIONS and CONDITIONS OF SALE

of

Green Hedges
PENN ROAD, BEACONSFIELD
BUCKINGHAMSHIRE

This Fine Detached Residence

with

A LODGE COTTAGE

and

NEARLY
3 ACRES
Formerly the home of the late "Enid Blyton"

FOR SALE BY PUBLIC AUCTION
(unless previously sold)
at "Green Hedges" Beaconsfield
on WEDNESDAY, 26th MAY, 1971, at 3.30 p.m.

Solicitors:
Messrs. J. D. LANGTON & PASSMORE
8 Bolton Street, Piccadilly, London, W1Y 8AU
Tel.: 01-499 2002 or 01-499 2316

Auctioneers:
...TON SWANNELL & SECRETT
...rade, Beaconsfield, Buckinghamshire
Tel.: Beaconsfield 2641/2
...ham, Little Chalfont, Chorleywood, Rickmansworth,
...od, London, W.5 and W.13

3

Green Hedges
at
BEACONSFIELD
BUCKINGHAMSHIRE.

Solicitors: Messrs. J. D. LANGTON & PASSMORE

Auctioneers:
HETHERINGTON
SWANNELL & SECRETT

Children of Adventures - The Main Series

ENID BLYTON was a highly successful series writer. Her consistent ability to 'come up trumps', had every children's publisher desperate to print her work.

At the height of her powers she was able to demand a straight 15 per cent royalty and complete negotiations at concept stage, insisting on a minimum print-run of 25,000 per volume without having written a word of the manuscript.

Enid was proud of her work, and she had full confidence in her ability to write stories that children loved to read. She tested the suitability of her work on children - perhaps more so that than any other author.

Through her magazines she constantly invited her young readers to write to her with their views and comments.

These were taken extremely seriously, and she spent much time reading and absorbing the thousands of letters she received. Children's reactions to her short stories in magazines such as *Sunny Stories*, meant that she was ideally placed to decide which stories to expand into full-length adventure books.

Just one successful series would have ensured her a prominent position in the history of children's literature - but she was able to do it time and time again.

Enid's predilection for producing series of books was not just good business, it was also good for her readers. Children require a variety of ideas and plots to stimulate their imagination - but they also like the security of the familiar. Enid was able to provide the delicate balance between familiarity and originality that encouraged children to read and read and read.

Part of the Famous Five series. Hodder & Stoughton, 1957. Illustrated by Eileen Soper.

*The first meeting of the Secret Seven. An illustration by Eileen Soper from **Secret of the Old Mill** published by Brockhampton in 1948.*

Enid spent many hours reading the children's reactions to her work. It placed her in an ideal position to decide which stories to develop into 'series'.

The Secret Series

The *Secret Island* was the first of five adventures shared by Jack, Mike, Nora and Peggy with Prince Paul joining them for the next four. This was Enid's first full-length adventure for older children, and the five books were illustrated by E.H.Davie, Harry Rountree, Eileen Soper and Dorothy Hall.

1. *The Secret Island*, 1938
2. *The Secret of Spiggy Holes*, 1940
3. *The Secret Mountain*, 1941
4. *The Secret of Killimooin*, 1943
5. *The Secret of Moon Castle*, 1953

The Secret of Spiggy Holes, published by Blackwell in 1940 with cover illustration by Harry Rountree (Interior illustrations by E.H.Davie).

The Secret Mountain, published by Blackwell in 1941 and illustrated by Harry Rountree.

The Secret of Killimooin, published by Blackwell in 1943 and illustrated by Eileen Soper.

The Secret of Moon Castle, published by Blackwell in 1953 and illustrated by Dorothy Hall. The last in the series.

The start of the serial in **Sunny Stories** *No.37, September 1937. Illustrated by E.H.Davie.*

Blackwell,1938. Illustrated by E.H.Davie. The second serial to be taken from **Sunny Stories** *and published as a book.* **Teachers World** *commented: 'Another example not only of Enid Blyton's ingenuity as a story writer but her incomparable gift of knowing just how young children like a story to be'.*

The Adventurous Four

Andy, a fourteen-year old fisher-boy, shares three adventures (two books and a short story) with Tom and his twin sisters Mary and Jill. The first book was one of only two that Enid wrote with a wartime setting, the other book *The Children of Kidillin*, written under the pseudonym of Mary Pollock, was also written in 1940 and both books are set in Scotland.

E.H. Davie illustrated the first book, with Jessie Land illustrating the second Adventurous Four book and the short story.

1. *The Adventurous Four*, 1941
2. *The Adventurous Four Again*, 1947

plus

'Off with the Adventurous Four Again!, *Enid Blyton's Omnibus*, 1952.

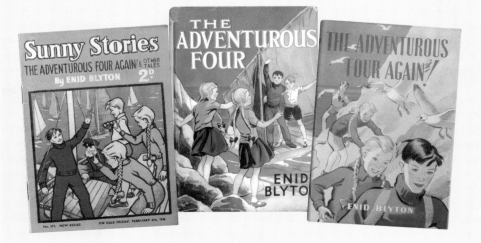

Left: **Sunny Stories** *No.373, February 1946. Illustrated by Jessie Land. Centre:* **The Adventurous Four,** *published by Newnes in 1941 and illustrated by E.H.Davie. Right:* **The Adventurous Four Again,** *published by Newnes in 1947 and illustrated by Jessie Land.*

Hodder & Stoughton, 1942.
Illustrated by Eileen Soper. First in the series.

Famous Five

The Famous Five are Julian, Dick, Anne and their cousin, Georgina Kirrin, who is known as George because she always wanted to be a boy. The fifth member is Timmy, George's pet dog. They first appeared in 1942, and their adventures featured in seven short stories and twenty-one books - the last being published in 1963. They were not just a British success, becoming popular in many European countries and further afield too.

Eight of the twenty-one books began as serials, the first of these being, *Five Go Off to Camp*, which appeared in *Sunny Stories*. The rest were featured either in her own magazine or *Princess*. The average length of a Famous Five novel turned out to be between 40,000 and 50,000 words and Enid was able to write it in four and a half days, a daily average of about 10,000 words or 1,500 words an hour. A truly amazing record.

The Five so much captured the affection of their readers, that many wrote to the publishers, Hodder and Stoughton, to suggest the formation of a Famous Five club. Enid agreed on the condition that the club should serve some useful purpose and suggested that it might help raise funds for a Shaftesbury Society Babies' home in Beaconsfield.

The club was formed in 1952, and with a peak membership of well over 200,000 children, it raised enough money to help other charities, such as the Great Ormond Street Hospital for Sick Children and Stoke Mandeville Hospital. This resulted in an 'Enid Blyton bed' named in her honour at Great Ormond Street, and a special 'Famous Five Ward' at Beaconsfield.

The Five appeared in a play at the Princes Theatre, London in 1955 and the success was repeated the following year at the London Hippodrome. They were adapted for cinema in 1957 and 1964. More recently there have been two television series (in the 1970s and 1990s) and a touring stage musical in 1997.

Hodder & Stoughton, 1964.
Eileen Soper's final Famous Five illustration.

Sunny Stories No.426, March 1948. Cover illustration by Eileen Soper. The only magazine cover to feature The Famous Five.

By the time Enid had written the last book in the series over six million Famous Five books had sold - and with each year the number increased at a staggering rate. When paperback editions were brought out these boosted sales by some sixty thousand on each title annually.

1. *Five on a Treasure Island*, 1942
2. *Five Go Adventuring Again*, 1943
3. *Five Run Away Together*, 1944
4. *Five Go to Smuggler's Top*, 1945
5. *Five Go Off in a Caravan*, 1946
6. *Five on Kirrin Island Again*, 1947
7. *Five Go Off to Camp*, 1948
8. *Five Get Into Trouble*, 1949
9. *Five Fall Into Adventure*, 1950
10. *Five on a Hike Together*, 1951
11. *Five Have a Wonderful Time*, 1952
12. *Five Go Down to the Sea*, 1953
13. *Five Go to Mystery Moor*, 1954
14. *Five Have Plenty of Fun*, 1955
15. *Five on a Secret Trail*, 1956
16. *Five Go to Billycock Hill*, 1957
17. *Five Get into a Fix*, 1958
18. *Five on Finniston Farm*, 1960
19. *Five Go to Demon's Rocks*, 1961
20. *Five Have a Mystery to Solve*, 1962
21. *Five are Together Again*, 1963
plus
'A Lazy Afternoon', *Magazine Annual* No.1, 1954
'George's Hair is too Long!', *Magazine Annual* No.2, 1955
'Five - and a Half-Term Adventure', *Magazine Annual* No. 3, 1956
Well Done Famous Five , Weeties, Australia, 1956
'When Timmy Chased the Cat', *Magazine Annual* No.4, 1957
'Good Old Timmy', *Princess Gift Book for Girls*, 1960
'Happy Christmas, Five!', *Princess Gift Book for Girls 1962*, 1961

George's dog, Timothy.

Hodder & Stoughton, 1948. Illustrated by Eileen Soper.

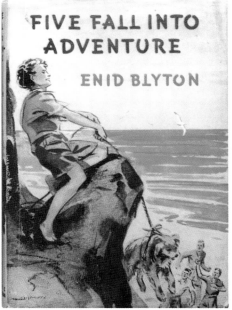

Hodder & Stoughton, 1950. Illustrated by Eileen Soper.

Hodder & Stoughton, 1954. Illustrated by Eileen Soper.

Hodder & Stoughton, 1960. Illustrated by Eileen Soper.

Hodder & Stoughton, 1963. Illustrated by Eileen Soper. Last in the series.

Programme for the Famous Five play, 1955.

FIVE AT FINNISTON FARM

The Five Are All Together Again!

"PHEW!" said Julian, mopping his wet forehead. "What a ...! Let's go and live at Equator—it would be compared to this!" ... stood leaning on his ..., out of breath with ... steep ride up a hill. ... grinned at him. ... out of training, ... said. "Let's sit ... a bit and look at ... We're pretty

... their bi- ... a nearby ... , their backs ... Below them ... ntryside, ... he day, ...

that she was taking paying guests at her farm-house—and had asked her to recommend visitors to her. George had promptly said she would like to go there with her

the bottom."

"There's the bus!" said Dick, as he heard the noise of a bus rumbling along in the distance. "Look, here it comes. We'll follow it."

ice-cream? There's a sh... over there that sells the... And I've got a sud... longing for nice ... plums!"

"You haven't s... word to Timmy yet, ... George, half - off... "He's been trotting ... you and licking you... —and he's so dr... hot and thirsty!"

"Shake paws, ... said Dick, and ... politely put up ... paw. He shook ... Julian, too, ... promptly ... careering ab... knocking ... on a bicycle.

"Come o... cream...

The very first issue of **Princess**, *January 1st., 1960.*
'Five at Finniston Farm'. Illustration by Eric Parker.

Illustrator Eileen Soper with her dog, in her garden at 'Wildings', Welwyn, Herts. She is mostly remembered for her illustrations to The Famous Five, although she produced much artwork for Enid'

As the series progressed the illustrator Eileen Soper, made the children look older - although they didn't seem to age at all in Enid's text.
The first is an illustration from **Five on a Treasure Island**, *1942 and the second is from* **Five on Finniston Farm**, *1960.*

Five on Kirrin Island Again published by Hodder & Stoughton in 1947 and illustrated by Eileen Soper. Although Enid checked artwork thoroughly, this one slipped through the net past editors, proof-readers and printers. The telescope was drawn the wrong way round by Eileen Soper and had to be corrected for later editions.

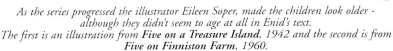

A LETTER FROM GEORGE

HALLO, CHILDREN!

I'm George. You know me, don't you? You know a lot of the adventures, too, that I've had with the others—Julian, Dick and Anne, my cousins. And of course you know old Timmy, my dog. The others call him *their* dog, too, but he isn't really. He's all mine, but I share him.

I've heard about the Famous Five Club. *I* want to wear a badge, too—after all, my head is on the badge, isn't it, so I *ought* to wear it! I'm asking Enid Blyton if I can have one. I *shall* feel proud!

An adventure for you,
from
GEORGE.

Above: The Famous Five Club Badge. c.1950s.

Right: Famous Five Bookmark. c.early 1950s.

Do YOU belong to the FAMOUS FIVE CLUB? Have YOU got the FAMOUS FIVE BADGE? There are friends of the FAMOUS FIVE all over the world. Wear the F.F. badge and you will know each other at once.

Enid Blyton

will wear one too, so that you will know her.

See other side for instructions

The Famous Five Card Game by Pepys, 1951.

Concerning George...

In an unguarded moment, Enid admitted to Rosica Colin, her foreign agent, that the character of George was based on herself. In her autobiography Enid wrote: 'George is real, but she is grown-up now... The real George was short-haired, freckled, sturdy and snub-nosed. She was sulky, as George is too, but she isn't now.'

You all know George and Timmy in the "Famous Five" books. They were real too.

No. 45 Five on a Windy Day.
No. 46 Five Have a Wonderful Time.
No. 47 Five Fall into Adventure.
No. 48 Five on Holiday.

Packaging for Famous Five 'Bestime' jigsaw. 1957

Five Have A Wonderful Time - A Bestime Jigsaw, 1957.

The Redoubtable
'Mr. Goon,'
To Miss. Enid Blyton,

Yrs. Sincerely.
J. Abbey
15-6-49

Left: The redoubtable Mr. Goon of the Find-Outers
Mystery Series. Painted specially for Enid by Joseph
Abbey in 1948.
                        Photo: Gillian Baverstock.

Above, Top: **The Mystery of the Burnt Cottage**,
Methuen, 1943. Illustrated by Joseph Abbey. The first
of the Find-Outers books.

Above, Centre: **The Mystery of the Missing Necklace**,
Methuen, 1945. Illustrated by Joseph Abbey.

The Five Find-Outers Mystery Series

Frederick Algernon Trotteville, better known as Fatty, with Larry, Daisy, Pip and little Bets were the Find-Outers. Master of disguise Fatty, with his dog Buster at his side, was one of Enid's strongest characters. In fifteen books and two short stories they solved mysteries in and around the village of Peterswood and were a constant thorn in the side of P.C. Theophilus Goon.

Inspector Jenks in this series was based on a friend, Stephen Jenkins, who worked in the Buckinghamshire police force at the time. Whenever he got promoted his fictional counterpart was likewise honoured. Three illustrators were used - Joseph Abbey, Treyer Evans and Lilian Buchanan.

1. *The Mystery of the Burnt Cottage*, 1943
2. *The Mystery of the Disappearing Cat*, 1944

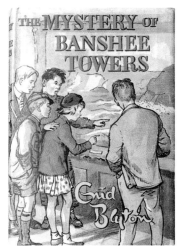

Methuen, 1951.
Illustrated by Treyer Evans.

Methuen, 1956.
Illustrated by Lilian Buchanan.

Methuen, 1957.
Illustrated by Lilian Buchanan.

Methuen, 1961.
Illustrated by Lilian Buchanan.
Last in the series.

Inspector Jenks in the Find-Outers Mystery series
was based on Enid's friend, Stephen Jenkins (right).

The Five Find-Outers,
with Buster the dog.
Clockwise from top left:
Daisy, Fatty, Bets, Larry,
Pip and Buster the dog.
Illustrated by J. Abbey,
1942.

Find Out!
The Enid Blyton Mystery
Game
by Pepys, 1958.

3. *The Mystery of the Secret Room,* 1945

4. *The Mystery of the Spiteful Letters,* 1946

5. *The Mystery of the Missing Necklace,* 1947

6. *The Mystery of the Hidden House,* 1948

7. *The Mystery of the Pantomime Cat,* 1949

8. *The Mystery of the Invisible Thief,* 1950

9. *The Mystery of the Vanished Prince,* 1951

10. *The Mystery of the Strange Bundle,* 1952

11. *The Mystery of Holly Lane,* 1953

12. *The Mystery of Tally-Ho Cottage,* 1954

13. *The Mystery of the Missing Man,* 1956

14. *The Mystery of the Strange Messages,* 1957

15. *The Mystery of Banshee Towers,* 1961

plus

'Just a Spot of Bother', *Chucklers Annual,* Australia, 1957

'The Five Find-Outers - and Dog Tackle the Mystery Sneak Thief', *June Book 1962,* 1961

The Adventure Series

The Adventure Series featured Jack, Lucy-Ann, Dinah, Philip and Kiki the parrot. Kiki was based on a real parrot that belonged to Enid's aunt.

The balding Bill Cunningham also had a real counterpart. He was a man Enid met while on holiday in Swanage. She found him amusing company and laughed when he suggested she put him in one of her books 'bald head and all'.

The Island of Adventure was the first in this series. Published in 1944 it contained Stuart Tresilian's excellent illustrations, which added additional atmosphere.

The Adventure books were extremely popular, and it amused Enid when one in the series was rejected by a new employee at Macmillan's, who had taken

the job fresh from university and hadn't heard of her.

1. *The Island of Adventure*, 1944
2. *The Castle of Adventure*, 1946
3. *The Valley of Adventure*, 1947
4. *The Sea of Adventure*, 1948
5. *The Mountain of Adventure*, 1949
6. *The Ship of Adventure*, 1950
7. *The Circus of Adventure*, 1952
8. *The River of Adventure*, 1955

Macmillan, 1946.
Illustrated by Stuart Tresilian.

Macmillan, 1948.
Illustrated by Stuart Tresilian.
Eileen Colwell wrote in her review,
"What hope has a band of
desperate men against four
children".

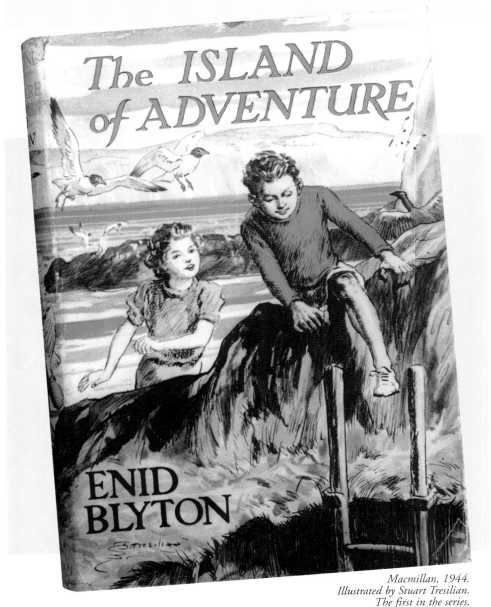

Macmillan, 1944.
Illustrated by Stuart Tresilian.
The first in the series.

The Caravan Family

Mike, Belinda and Ann were 1940s travellers as the family sold their house to live in a caravan. They do leave their caravan to travel on boats and it is in this series for younger readers that Enid covers two of her own cruises; in the Stella Polaris she went to Madeira *(The Pole Star Family)* and also a cruise to New York on the Queen Elizabeth. All six books were first serialised in *Playways* and an abridged version of *The Caravan Family* was serialised in *Wife and Home*, 1955-56, as 'Adventure Ahead!'. William Fyffe illustrated the first book and Ruth Gervis the rest.

1. *The Caravan Family*, 1945
2. *The Saucy Jane Family*, 1948
3. *The Pole Star Family*, 1950
4. *The Seaside Family*, 1950
5. *The Buttercup Farm Family*, 1951
6. *The Queen Elizabeth Family*, 1951

Lutterworth Press, 1945.
Illustrated by William Fyffe.
First in the series.

Lutterworth Press, 1948.
Illustrated by Ruth Gervis.

'The Seaside Family' in **Playways,** *July 1949 - A Caravan Family adventure. From March 1945 until the closure of the magazine in 1956, Enid contributed to all but one issue.*

Clockwise from above:
The Children at Happy House,
Shakespeare Head Press, 1946.
Illustrated by Kathleen M. Gell.
The Happy House Children Again,
Latimer House, 1955.
Cover illustration by Dorothy Brook.
Text illustrations by Kathleen Gell.
Benjy and the Others,
Latimer House, 1955.
Illustrated by Kathleen Gell.

The Happy House Children

The original two books about Jack, Jane and Benjy were joined by a third which was serialised in the final days of *Sunny Stories*. This series was aimed very much at younger children and relied heavily on Kathleen Gell's illustrations.

1. *The Children at Happy House*, 1946
2. *The Happy House Children Again*, 1947
3. *Benjy and the Others*, 1955

The Secret Seven

The Secret Seven was reportedly conceived when one of Enid Blyton's publishers, Ewart Wharmby of Brockhampton Press, casually mentioned that his children had formed a secret society in the shed at the bottom of his garden. Enid asked him for further details and as a result *The Secret Seven* was published in 1949.

However, this story may have become confused for Janet, Peter and their dog Scamper first appeared in 1947 in a small picture book - *At Seaside Cottage*, illustrated by Eileen Soper. Peter was seven and Janet a year younger. A year later in their next book, *Secret of the Old Mill*, they formed the Secret Seven with the addition of Pam, Colin, Jack, Barbara

and George. The first of many secret passwords was 'Tiddly-winks'!

The Secret Seven series proper consisted of fifteen books and five short stories written between 1949 and 1963. They were illustrated by George Brook, Bruno Kay and Burgess Sharrocks . Many of the books were first serialised in magazines and apart from her own journals they appeared in *Mickey Mouse Weekly*, *Princess*, and *School Friend*. Designed for younger children, the vocabulary was simpler than with other adventure stories.

1. *The Secret Seven*, 1949
2. *The Secret Seven Adventure*, 1950
3. *Well Done Secret Seven*, 1951
4. *Secret Seven on the Trail*, 1952
5. *Go Ahead Secret Seven*, 1953
6. *Good Work Secret Seven*, 1954

7. *Secret Seven Win Through*, 1955
8. *Three Cheers Secret Seven*, 1956
9. *Secret Seven Mystery*, 1957
10. *Puzzle for the Secret Seven*, 1958
11. *Secret Seven Fireworks*, 1959
12. *Good Old Secret Seven*, 1960
13. *Shock for the Secret Seven*, 1961
14. *Look Out Secret Seven*, 1962
15. *Fun for the Secret Seven*, 1963
plus
'The Humbug Adventure', *Magazine Annual* No.1, 1954
'Adventure on the Way Home', *Magazine Annual* No.2, 1955
'An Afternoon with the Secret Seven', *Magazine Annual* No.3, 1956
Where are the Secret Seven?, Weeties, Australia, 1956
'Hurry Secret Seven, Hurry!', *Magazine Annual* No.4, 1957

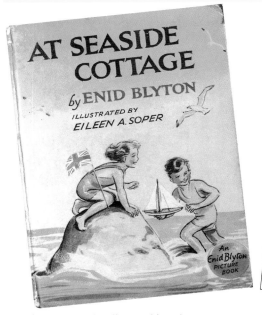

Brockhampton, 1947. Illustrated by Eileen Soper. Interior illustration on right features Janet, Peter and their dog, Scamper.

Brockhampton, 1948. Illustrated by Eileen Soper.

Brockhampton, 1949. Illustrated by George Brook. First in the series.

Brockhampton, 1950. Illustrated by George Brook.

Brockhampton, 1954. Illustrated by Bruno Kay.

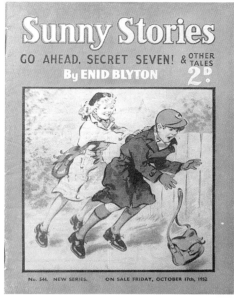

Sunny Stories No. 544, October 1952. The only issue to feature the Secret Seven on the cover.

Brockhampton, 1963. Illustrated by Burgess Sharrocks. Last in the series.

Mickey Mouse Weekly, July 21st., 1951.
Enid's first appearance in the comic. The Secret Seven appear in strip form illustrated by George Brook.

Left:
The Secret
Seven
Card Game
by Pepys,
1955.

Above: Secret Seven Jigsaw Puzzle by Bestime, 1954.

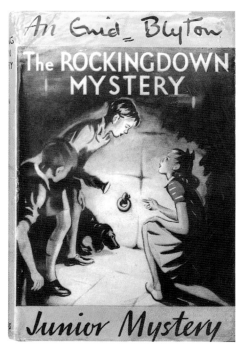

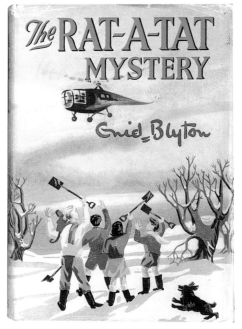

The Barney Mystery Series

The six books in this series were aimed at slightly older children. The adventures feature Roger, Diana and their cousin Snubby teamed up with Barney the circus boy and his monkey Miranda. Snubby's dog 'Loony' was based on Enid's own dog 'Laddie'.

The first book in the series, *The Rockingdown Mystery*, was part of the Collins Junior Mystery Series, and was intended as a one-off. But as with so many of Enid's books, her young readers just wanted more, and so it was developed into a series. Gilbert Dunlop illustrated all except the fifth book, which was illustrated by Anyon Cook.

1. *The Rockingdown Mystery*, 1949
2. *The Rilloby Fair Mystery*, 1950
3. *The Ring o' Bells Mystery*, 1951
4. *The Rubadub Mystery*, 1952
5. *The Rat-a-tat Mystery*, 1956
6. *The Ragamuffin Mystery*, 1959

Top Left: Published by Collins, 1949. Illustrated by Gilbert Dunlop. The first in the series.
Centre Left: Published by Collins, 1950. Illustrated by Gilbert Dunlop.
Top Right: Published by Collins, 1956. Illustrated by Anyon Cook.
Centre Right: Published by Collins, 1959. Illustrated by Gilbert Dunlop. Last in the series.

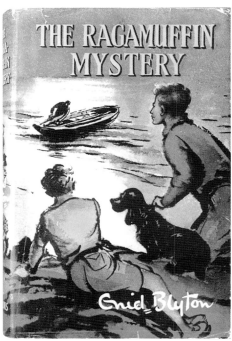

*A Barney & Friends postcard from the late 50s sent by Enid in 1964 to her nephew, Carey, regarding their collaboration on a joint book, **Mixed Bag**.*

*A Swedish version of **Well Done Secret Seven**, 1965.*

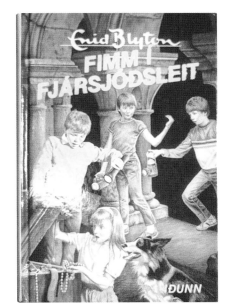

Icelandic edition of the Famous Five series, 1974.

*A French edition of **The Mystery of the Vanished Prince**, 1964.*

*A French version of **Five Go Down To The Sea**, 1966.*

Enid Blyton's books have averaged sales of ten million a year. Of these, five to six million sell abroad. Displayed here are just a few of the foreign language editions.

*A Swedish edition of **The Secret of Moon Castle**, 1970.*

*A Flemish version of **The Mystery of the Strange Bundle**, 1970.*

*Unlike their English counterparts the French editions of Enid's Mystery and Adventure books had colour illustrations inside. This one by Jean Sidobre for **Five On A Secret Trail**, 1968.*

*A German edition of **Five Run Away Together**, undated.*

43

ENID wrote approximately thirty one-off full-length books, including some exciting adventure stories that rank among her best work. Each book involved completely separate characters. Although they were not series, for convenience they can be split into four groups:

'Pot Pourri' - Adventures from Various Publishers

Enid's first full-length book, not to originate from a serial, was the *Boys' and Girls' Circus Book*. Apart from the Adventure Series this was her longest book, and it tells the story of how Pip and Susy-Ann with their pet goat Mr Binks run away to join Mr Phillipino's Circus. Also in this group are *The Treasure Hunters*, about the search for the lost fortune of the Grayling family, *The Boy Next Door*, which tells of the attempted kidnapping of a young American boy, Kit, by his wicked uncle, and *Adventure of the Strange Ruby*, which, set in the area around Corfe Castle in Dorset, is one of the few Blyton books to have a precise location.

1. *Boys' and Girls' Circus Book*, News Chronicle, 1939
2. *The Treasure Hunters*, Newnes, 1940
3. *The Boy Next Door*, Newnes, 1944
4. *Come to the Circus!*, Newnes, 1948
5. *Holiday House*, Evans, 1955
6. *Adventure of the Strange Ruby*, Brockhampton, 1960
7. *The Mystery That Never Was*, Collins, 1961

Newnes Mary Pollock Books

One reviewer wrote that 'Enid Blyton had better look to her laurels', when this popular group of six books of assorted stories was published under the pseudonym Mary Pollock, in the early 1940s. A decade later they were republished by Werner Laurie under Enid's own name.

1. *Three Boys and a Circus*, 1940
2. *The Children of Kidillin*, 1940
3. *The Adventures of Scamp*, 1943
4. *The Secret of Cliff Castle*, 1943
5. *Mischief at St. Rollo's*, 1943
6. *Smuggler Ben*, 1943

Lutterworth Family Books

These all revolve around families with a problem, and there is a strong moral tone in the manner that they cope with their various misfortunes.

1. *The Family at Red Roofs*, 1945
2. *Hollow Tree House*, 1945
3. *The Put-Em-Rights*, 1946
4. *House-at-the-Corner*, 1947
5. *Those Dreadful Children*, 1949
6. *The Six Bad Boys*, 1951
7. *The Children at Green Meadows*, 1954

Lutterworth Younger Adventures

Playways serialised a number of adventures for younger children and on the magazine's closure in 1956, Blyton stories continued to appear in Annuals for another ten years. All were published as books by Lutterworth. The final one, *The Hidey Hole*, published in August 1964, was Enid's last full-length fictional work.

1. *The Very Big Secret*, 1952
2. *Snowball the Pony*, 1953
3. *The Adventure of the Secret Necklace*, 1954
4. *Run-About's Holiday*, 1955
5. *Four in a Family*, 1956
6. *The Birthday Kitten*, 1958
7. *The Four Cousins*, 1962
8. *The Boy Who Wanted a Dog*, 1963
9. *The Hidey Hole*, 1964

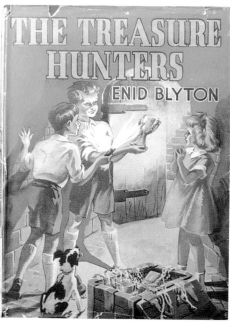

Newnes, 1940. Illustrated by Edith Wilson and Joyce Davies.

Newnes, 1944. Illustrated by Alfred E. Bestall (now known for illustrating Rupert Bear).

Brockhampton, 1960. Illustrated by Roger Payne.

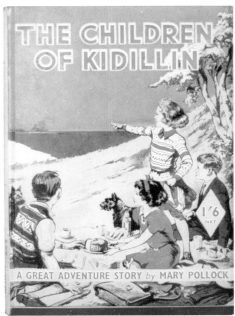

Newnes, 1940. Illustrated by Edith Wilson

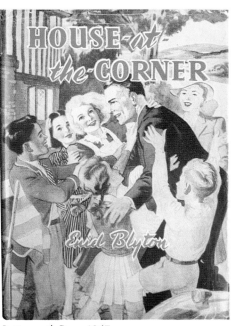

Lutterworth Press, 1947.
Illustrated by Elsie Walker.

Lutterworth Press, 1956.
Illustrated by Tom Kerr.

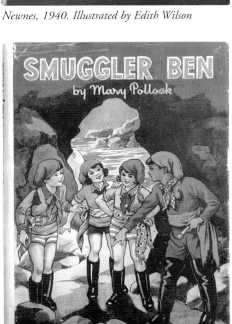

Written under the name of Mary Pollock. Newnes,
second edition, 1945. Illustrated by E.H.Davie.

Lutterworth Press, second edition, 1949.
Cover by Barbara Freeman.

Lutterworth Press, 1958.
Illustrated by Grace Lodge.

Republished by Werner Laurie, 1950.
Illustrated by G.W.Backhouse.

Lutterworth Press, 1954.
Illustrated by Grace Lodge.

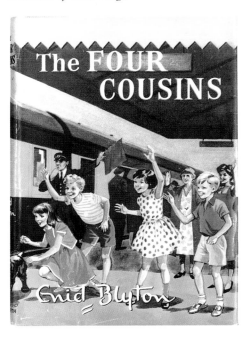

Lutterworth Press, 1962.
Illustrated by Joan Thompson.

Back to School

MANY critics considered Enid's school stories to be amongst her best constructed work. She wrote, between 1940 and 1951, a total of sixteen school novels, centred round Whyteleafe, St Clare's, St Rollo's and Malory Towers. All were boarding schools - two were girls' only and two co-educational.

The schools seemed to successfully iron out the flaws of all but the most turbulent inmates. Illnesses, runaways, midnight feasts and tricks against French mistresses - all featured prominently.

Whyteleafe

Newnes, 1940
Illustrated by W. Lindsay Cable.

Whyteleafe is run by two women, Miss Belle and Miss Best, with supporting male and female teachers. Elizabeth Allen was determined to be the naughtiest girl in this school. Written at a time when authors such as Elinor Brent-Dyer and Angela Brazil were at the height of their popularity, this first attempt at a school story by Enid was very different. Whyteleafe was a progressive co-educational school where pocket money was shared out equally and punishments were decided by the children themselves at school meetings. There were three books, the first two illustrated by W. Lindsay Cable and the third by Kenneth Lovell, and a short story came later illustrated by Bruno Kay.

Newnes, 1942
Illustrated by W. Lindsay Cable.

1. *The Naughtiest Girl in the School*, 1940
2. *The Naughtiest Girl Again*, 1942
3. *The Naughtiest Girl is a Monitor*, 1945
plus
'Here's the Naughtiest Girl Again!', *Enid Blyton's Omnibus*, 1952

St Clare's

The six St Clare's books followed the progress of Pat and Isabel O'Sullivan up the school and we see them transformed from spoilt brats into jolly good eggs!

Their first year is dealt with in detail in the first three books and following years get a book each. Readers may have felt slightly cheated that the series ended

Methuen, 1941. The First in the series
Illustrated by W. Lindsay Cable.

before they got into their final year (except in Germany where a further twelve books were added to fill in gaps and finish off!) As the series went on a number of powerful central characters emerged and the O'Sullivan twins were at times only playing a background role. W.Lindsay Cable illustrated the series and the similarity between many of the girls in his illustrations was due to his fondness for using his wife to model most of the poses!

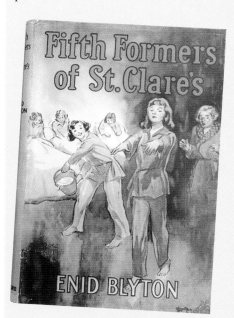

Methuen, 1945.
Illustrated by W. Lindsay Cable.
Last in the series.

1. *The Twins at St Clare's*, 1941
2. *The O'Sullivan Twins*, 1942
3. *Summer Term at St Clare's*, 1943
4. *The Second Form at St Clare's*, 1944
5. *Claudine at St Clare's*, 1944
6. *Fifth Formers of St Clare's*, 1945

St Rollo's

Mischief at St Rollo's was a one-off school story written under the pseudonym of Mary Pollock in 1943. Aimed at a slightly younger age group than the other school stories, it nevertheless has all the usual ingredients skilfully mixed in the blender. Janet and Michael are the two central characters who arrive at their new school and the book tells the story of their highly

Werner Laurie, 1952.
Illustrated by C.Holland.

adventurous first term there. Hilda McGavin illustrated the first edition and in 1952 it was released under Enid's own name with illustrations by C. Holland.

Malory Towers

Darrell Rivers goes from bottom to top in this school series. Enid based the quick-tempered heroine, Darrell Rivers, on herself and the name is a play on Darrell Waters, her second husband. He, like the fictional Darrell's father, was also a surgeon.

Methuen, 1946.
Illustrated by Stanley Lloyd.
First in the series.

Malory Towers is run on stricter lines than Enid's other schools, although it shares with them all the favourite boarding school situations. The arrival of Darrell's younger sister, Felicity, halfway through the series, enables us to look at the school at two levels as we follow the progress of them both. Unlike St Clare's the readers were treated to a book in each year and this time the final year was included. (The Germans managed to add a further ten books to this series as well!). Stanley Lloyd illustrated all six books, which had their dustwrappers updated in the mid 1950s by Lilian Buchanan.

Methuen, 1947.
Illustrated by Stanley Lloyd.

Methuen, 1948.
Illustrated by Stanley Lloyd.

1. *First Term at Malory Towers*, 1946
2. *The Second Form at Malory Towers*, 1947
3. *The Third Year at Malory Towers*, 1948
4. *Upper Fourth at Malory Towers*, 1949
5. *In the Fifth at Malory Towers*, 1950
6. *Last Term at Malory Towers*, 1951

Enid Blyton's own character notes for the Malory Towers series. Used to ensure continuity.

Roll Up! Roll Up! Come to the Circus!

THE popularity of the circus was at its peak during the 1940s and 1950s. Every town looked forward to its arrival, with the raz-ma-taz of clowns, acrobats, performing animals, and death defying feats of the flying trapeze. It was a real treat for the family and no one enjoyed the performance more than the children.

It is of little surprise that Enid Blyton brought the romance of the circus into children's reading. With a series, three full-length books and a handful of shorter ones, children were able to ride bare-back with Lotta in Mr Galliano's Circus or enter the ring with Willie and his clever goose, Cackles, in Mr Carl Crack's Circus. They could also share the excitement of the first night performances of Jimmy with his dog, Lucky, Fenella with her little bear, Bobbo, and Pip with his wonderful animal noises. With cheeky chimps, Grin and Bearit, and saucy elephants, Rag, Tag and Bobtail there was never a dull moment on the road with the circus.

An illustration by
Eileen Soper from
Come to the Circus,
Brockhampton, 1943.

Mr. Galliano's Circus Series:

1. *Mr Galliano's Circus*, 1938
2. *Hurrah for the Circus!*, 1939
3. *Circus Days Again*, 1942
plus
All About The Circus, 1939
'A Circus Adventure', *Enid Blyton's
Omnibus*, 1952

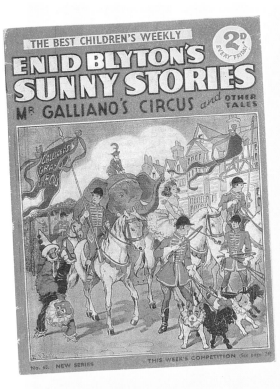

*Sunny Stories No.65, April 1938.
Illustrated by E.H.Davie.*

*Mr. Galliano's Circus,
published by Newnes in
1938 and illustrated by
E.H.Davie. It is
rumoured that the bones
of this story come from
Enid's attempt at an
adult novel written and
rejected a few years
earlier. However it seems
more likely that she used
this book in the **Boys'
and Girls' Circus Book**
about Mr Phillipino's
Circus. This was
published in the middle
of the Galliano series by
the **News Chronicle**,
who up to this point had
only published recycled
material. Enid was never
one to waste an idea.*

Left: **Mr. Galliano**, a jigsaw produced by Bestime in 1948. It was one of a set of four, which were the first Blyton character jigsaws.

Left: **Come to the Circus**, Brockhampton, 1943. Illustrated by Eileen Soper. It is the only Blyton title to be used on two completely different books, published within five years of each other in 1943 and 1948. Right: Newnes, 1948. Illustrated by Joyce Johnson.

Sunny Stories No. 399, February 1947. Cover illustrated by Joyce Johnson.

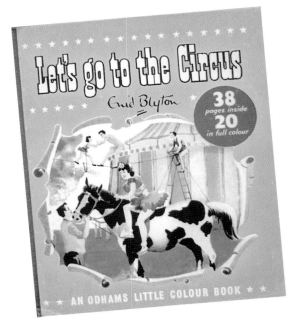

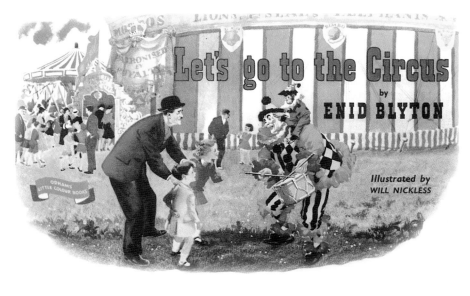

The cover (left) and the title page (right) of **Let's go to the Circus**, illustrated by Will Nickless. Odhams, 1951.

Enid and the Animals

ENID was fond of writing about animals. She kept pets at Old Thatch and at Green Hedges, and many of these seemingly inherited their owner's literary talents. It all began with Bobs, a fox-terrier, who wrote his first letter in *Teachers World* in September 1929.

After this there was no stopping him and there were weekly letters from this dog for the next sixteen years. Occasionally he had a sore paw or was away at the vet's and then Sandy, another fox-terrier, took over the job. But Bobs had undoubted stamina and even a minor set back such as his death in 1935 did not halt the flow. He had three volumes of letters published privately, the first in 1933 and two posthumously in 1937 and 1940. All sold in their thousands.

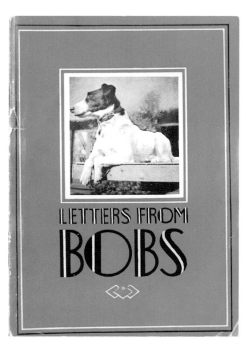

Privately published, 1933.

Not to be outdone Bimbo, a Siamese cat, took up the challenge in June 1940, by exercising his claws on a weekly letter in *Sunny Stories*. In June 1942 Topsy, a new fox-terrier, came in on the action and for the

next four years alternated with Bimbo. In 1946 the workload was spread further still as almost anything at Green Hedges that could walk, fly, crawl or swim joined in the fun.

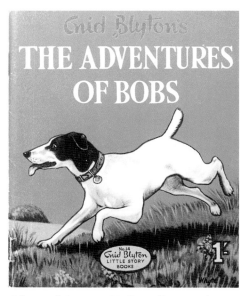

Johnston & Bacon, 1955. Cover illustration by Whyte. Text illustrations by MacDowell.

Bobs had a book named after him, though the story was clearly about another dog. There was also a book published in 1943 titled *Bimbo and Topsy*. This was about the fictitious adventures they shared with Gillian,

Newnes, 1943. Illustrated by Lucy Gee.

Imogen and Mummy (Enid). Cosy, a fat tabby, and a re-incarnated Bobs also played their part.

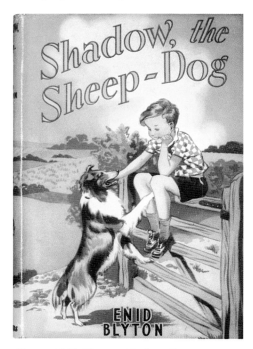

Newnes, 1942. Illustrated by Lucy Gee.

In the early 1940s Enid wrote two books about fictional dogs, Shadow and Scamp. Shadow the sheep-dog shares in all sorts of adventures with his young master Johnny, who was given him as a pup. Perhaps this is Enid's answer to Lassie, who was very much in vogue at the time. Scamp is a terrier belonging to Joan and Kenneth Hill, whose adventures were

Left: Newnes, 1943. Written under the name of Mary Pollock. Right: Re-published by Werner Laurie in 1955. Cover illustration by Leonardo. Text illustrations by Olive Openshaw.

recounted in one of the books written under the pseudonym of Mary Pollock.

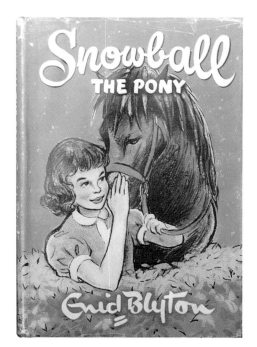

Lutterworth Press, 1953. Illustrated by Iris Gillespie.

Ten years later she wrote *Snowball the Pony*, a book for younger readers about an inappropriately named black pony belonging to Willie, Sheila and Timmy. Later still came a series of three books about a kitten.

These were made up from a series of photographs by Paul Kaye about a kitten called Tinker and the various

Harvill Press, 1955. Photographs: Paul Kaye.

pranks he gets up to with Floppy, a puppy. Enid provided a very simple text.

Large animals not so suitable for pets were also written about in accounts of visits to the zoo, both non-fictional and fictional.

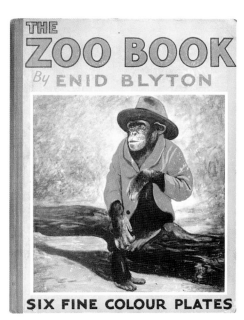

Newnes,1926. Cover artist unknown.

One of the earliest books for Newnes was *The Zoo Book*, the commissioning of which sparked off the romance with her first husband, Hugh.

In fiction there was *The Smith Family at the Zoo*, a reader for E.J.Arnold and even the odd 'cartoon' character paid a visit, as in the 1958 book for Sandle's, *Scamp Goes to the Zoo*.

Sandle's, 1958. Illustrated by Pierre Probst.

Newnes, 1938. Illustrated by Kathleen Nixon.

Birn Brothers, c.1927. Illustrator unknown.

J.Coker, 1952. Text illustrated by Douglas Cuthill.

Evans, 1929. Text illustrations by Denis King and Enid Blyton.

Evans, 1934.
Illustrator unknown.

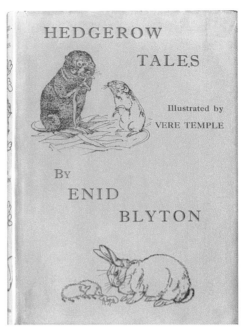

Methuen, 1935.
Illustrated by Vere Temple.

Evans, 1944. Cover illustration by Noel Hopking. Text illustrated by Donia Nachshen.

Evans, 1940. Illustrator unknown.

J.Coker, 1952.
Text illustrated by Douglas Cuthill.

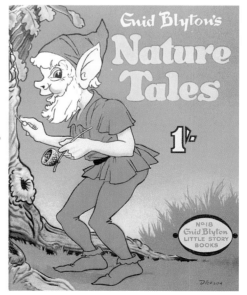

Johnston & Bacon, 1957. Cover illustration by Dickson. Text illustrated by Douglas Cuthill.

HAD Enid remained a teacher, one of her favourite subjects would have undoubtedly been Natural History. A love of nature was encouraged at an early age by her father and some of her earliest writing for *Teachers World* was her weekly nature lessons, which collectively formed a course of study. In the years that followed, *Teachers World* published two further courses, *Round the Year with Enid Blyton* and *Hedgerow Tales*.

All three courses were published in book form, the first two by Evans and the third by Methuen. In the 1940s and 1950s she wrote a series of thirty-six Nature Readers for Macmillan, all wonderfully illustrated by Eileen Soper, who also painted a series of sixty nature plates to accompany the text. Enid also produced a number of slightly less academic books on various aspects of nature

COUNTRY CORNER "BUSY BEES"

WHAT a busy month this is for us, the humming bees! You can see us all day long, hurrying here and there, carrying nectar from the flowers to make into sweet honey in our hives.

The flowers give us honey. What do we bees do in return? We act as postmen for the flowers, and carry their pollen from one to another, so that they can make seed. Did you know that?

Look at us as we go into a flower. We come out dusted with yellow pollen! Off we go and take it to the next flower, and leave some there. Then that flower can begin to make seed, because it has another flower's pollen to help it.

So you see, we do not take our honey and give nothing in return! We work for the flowers—and they work for us by making us their sweet nectar.

And *we* work for you, because you eat our honey.

Good Housekeeping, July 1947.
Illustration by Stanley Jackson.

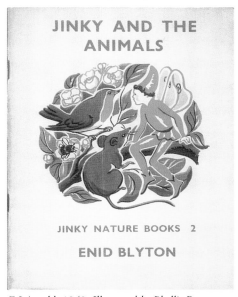

E.J.Arnold, 1948. Illustrated by Phyllis Denton.

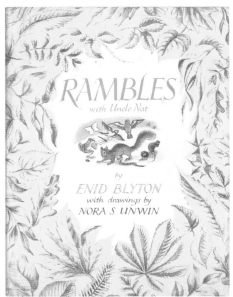

National Magazine Co., 1947. Illustrated by Nora S. Unwin.

Macmillan, 1953. Illustrated by Eileen Soper.

Evans, 1952. Illustrated by Eileen Soper.

53

Down At The Farm

ENID enjoyed writing about farms. With names such as Appletree, Cherry Tree, Willow, Mistletoe and Buttercup, they conjured up a picturesque image of an idyllic world, where children could marvel at day old chicks and watch new born lambs frolicking. Farmyards were inviting places and not somewhere where one waddled in wellies up to one's knees in it!

Apart from two series set on farms there were also some picture books. The Famous Five enjoyed many a sumptuous spread, laid on in a farm kitchen by a rosy-cheeked farmer's wife who invariably had a twinkle in her eye. The Caravan Family had their wanderings interrupted, whilst they spent a holiday on Buttercup Farm and Philip, Jack, Dinah and Lucy-Ann enjoyed splendid hospitality in an unpronounceable Welsh farm before disappearing into the 'Mountain of Adventure'.

Enid even bought her own farm in her beloved Dorset. Named Manor Farm at Stourton Caundle. Although Enid and her husband never lived there, she and Kenneth paid visits whilst on their golfing holidays in nearby Swanage. It provided the inspiration for Finniston Farm in the eighteenth Famous Five Book.

The Farm Series:
1. *The Children of Cherry Tree Farm*, 1940
2. *The Children of Willow Farm*, 1942
3. *More Adventures on Willow Farm*, 1943

Six Cousins Series:
1. *Six Cousins at Mistletoe Farm*, 1948
2. *Six Cousins Again*, 1950

Country Life, 1940. Illustrated by Harry Rountree. Rory, Sheila, Benjy and Penny leave London to go and first stay, then live on a farm. Billed as a countryside story, it is very much a 'back to nature' novel, that resulted in a series of three books.

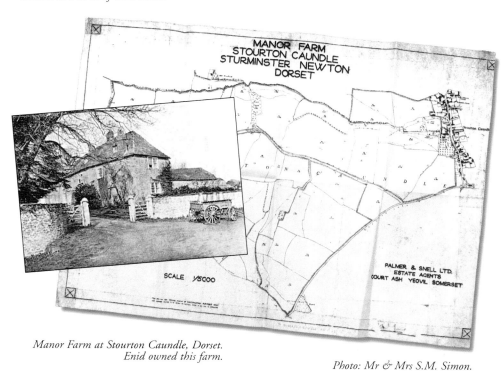

*Manor Farm at Stourton Caundle, Dorset.
Enid owned this farm.*

Photo: Mr & Mrs S.M. Simon.

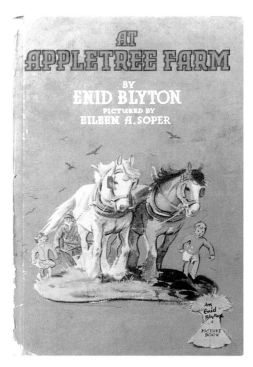

*The cover (centre) and two illustrations by Eileen Soper from **At Appletree Farm**, published by Brockhampton in 1944.*

Country Life, 1942. Illustrated by Harry Rountree.

Evans, 1948. Illustrated by Peter Beigel. In this book the horses are almost as important as the two lots of feuding cousins. Enid dedicated the novel to her daughter, Imogen, who was at the time recovering from polio.

Sampson Low, 1951. Illustrated by Cicely Steed.

Cartoon and other Short Story Characters

SUNNY STORIES and *Enid Blyton's Magazine* featured many cartoon and other short story characters. Topping the list was Brer Rabbit, who originally featured in short stories by the American author, Joel Chandler Harris.

Sunny Stories for Little Folks, No.2, July 1926. Cover illustration by Ernest Aris.

Sunny Stories in two series spanned twenty-seven years with a total of 803 magazines. During this period there were 217 Brer Rabbit stories, all but one illustrated by Ernest Aris - Hilda McGavin was responsible for the one. There were, of course, many more Brer Rabbit stories written by Enid in *Teachers World* and later in *Enid Blyton's Magazine* and a number of the stories have been collected in eighteen books, with Grace Lodge providing all the later illustrating.

Altogether about thirty characters or groups of characters made the transition to book form. Most of these had started life either in *Sunny Stories* or in other periodicals where Enid had a regular 'spot' - and all but five were under way before the end of the 1940s. Some characters like Simple Simon (in both *Teachers*

Sunny Stories for Little Folks, No.43, April 1928 Cover illustration by Joan Hoyle

World and *Sunny Stories*) and the dog and cat duo, Bundle and Cosy (in the *Sunday Dispatch* and also in *Daily Mail* Annuals) never made it to book form, whilst another, Mr Wumble, was only used in an Old Thatch reader.

Sunny Stories for Little Folks, No.44, April 1928.

The Hackett, Collins and Sandle's series of the mid and late 1950s included some familiar names such as Bimbo, Scamp and Bobs, but were translations of books previously

Both titles published by Collins, 1955. Both illustrated by Pierre Probst.

published in France and it seems likely that Enid did little other than lend her name to these books. The John and Mary Series of nine books published by Brockhampton in the late 1960s were previously published short stories with name changes to make it appear like a new series. This was probably done by an editor because by this time Enid was already in a poor state of health.

Brockhampton, 1968. Illustrated by Jacques Fromont.

Brockhampton, 1957. Illustrated by Fred White.

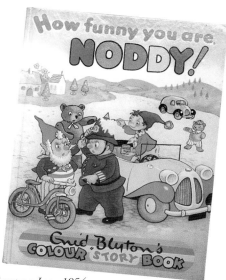

Many of these 'character' books are inevitably collections of short stories. Some characters appeared in picture strip form and although these were mostly full-length stories, without the pictures they would have been brief. Leading the way is Mary Mouse who starred in twenty-six books (twenty-three strip books, two painting books and a novelty cut-out book) and Josie, Click and Bun and Clicky also featured in a number of books.

Sampson Low, 1954.

Brockhampton, 1954. Illustrated by Molly Brett.

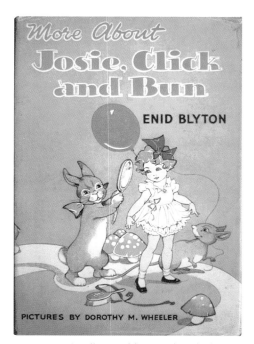

Newnes, 1948. Illustrated by Dorothy Wheeler.

Brockhampton, 1963. Illustrated by R. Paul-Höye.

Only two cartoon characters have had a series of 'proper' books written about them - Bom and Noddy. Bom was actually the last of the characters to emerge and there were fourteen Bom books of various different types, though only eight of these were full-length books.

Brer Rabbit *(18 books, the first in 1925, and numerous uncollected short stories)*

Brer Rabbit's first appearance under Enid's name was in a Nelson reader as part of their Reading Practice Series. She also wrote a number of stories in various Cassell's Annuals in the 1920s. From then on Brer Rabbit and Brer Fox were to trick each other over the next three decades.

Newnes, 1938. Illustrated by Kathleen Nixon.

Johnston & Bacon, 1955.
Cover illustration by Dickson.
Text illustrated by Peacock.

Latimer House, 1957. Illustrated by Grace Lodge.

Binkle and Flip *(1 book, first published in 1925, and some short stories).*

Enid wrote six short stories about two bad bunnies, Sandy and Bill in 1924, but they weren't published at the time. Six months later she added a few more and *The Book of Bunnies* came out in 1925. By this time their names had been changed to Binkle and Flip, to add a more rabbitty flavour. Kathleen Nixon illustrated the book and Ernest Aris the short stories.

Newnes, 1950.
Illustrated by
Kathleen
Nixon.

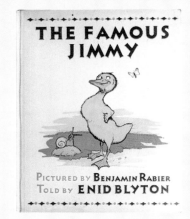

Newnes, 1951. Illustrated by Ernest Aris

Hop, Skip and Jump *(1 book, first published in 1926, and some short stories).*

These were three brownies who made their debut in *The Book of Brownies* and subsequently various appearances in *Sunny Stories* in the 1920s, all illustrated by Ernest Aris.

Feefo, Tuppeny and Jinks *(1 book, first published in 1935).*

They were the stars of *The Green Goblin Book* published by Newnes in 1935, but they only achieved star billing in the Staples Press reprint in 1951. For some strange reason Tuppeny got promoted over Feefo in the later Collins edition.

Above: Staples Press, 1951.
Illustrated by Norman Meredith.

Right: Collins, 1967.
Illustrated by Hilda McGavin.

Jimmy *(1 book, first published in 1936).*

Jimmy was an amazing duckling whose adventures took place in the farmyard. The one book is dedicated to all those who love ducklings and especially Gillian and Imogen. Benjamin Rabier was the illustrator.

Frederick Muller, 1936. Illustrated by Benjamin Rabier.

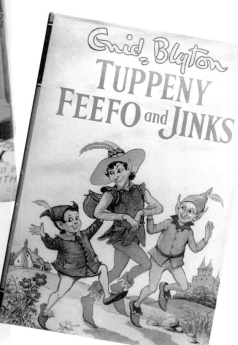

Billy-Bob *(1 book, first published in 1938, and many short stories).*

Billy-Bob is a merry little boy with curly red hair, a fat younger sister called Belinda and a dog called Wags. His everyday adventures appeared both in *Teachers World* and *Sunny Stories*, where he was always illustrated by Dorothy Wheeler. May Smith illustrated the one book in which some of the stories were collected.

Far Right: **Billy-Bob Tales**
Methuen, 1938.
Illustrated by May Smith.

Right: **Sunny Stories**, *No.56,*
February 1938.
Cover Illustration by Dorothy Wheeler.

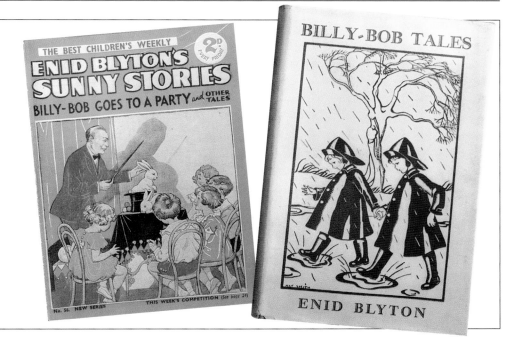

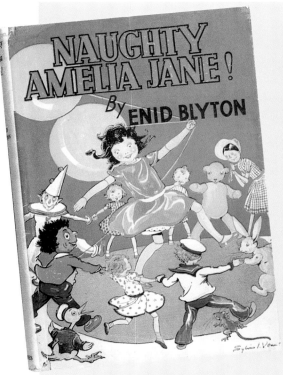

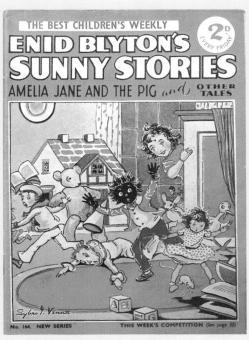

Amelia Jane *(3 books, the first in 1939, and further short stories).*

The naughty rag doll Amelia Jane was based on the doll owned by Enid's daughter, Gillian. The doll featured in many stories in *Sunny Stories*, some of which were collected into books. Sylvia Venus was the illustrator.

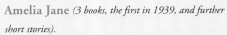

Right: This doll belonged to Enid's daughter, Gillian, and was the inspiration for Naughty Amelia Jane.

Covers displayed above from left to right:

Naughty Amelia Jane !
Newnes, 1939. Illustrated by Sylvia Venus.

Sunny Stories *No.164, March 1940.*
Cover illustrated by Sylvia Venus.

More About Amelia Jane !
Newnes, 1954. Illustrated by Sylvia Venus.

Mister Meddle *(3 books, the first in 1940, and further short stories)*

He is a pixie who is always sticking his nose into other people's business, resulting in comical situations. Joyce Mercer and Rosalind Turvey shared the illustrating credits in all three books making him one of the few characters to have two illustrators involved at the same time.

Josie, Click and Bun *(5 books, the first in 1940, and other short stories)*

They are a doll, a mouse and a rabbit whose adventures graced the centre pages of *Sunny Stories* in picture strip form. There were five books all delightfully illustrated by Dorothy Wheeler.

Betsy-May *(1 book, first published in 1940, and many short stories)*

The fly-leaf to the book of collected stories says that Betsy-May is a small girl who is naughty, lovable, kind, awkward, unexpected - exactly like everybody's child! She sounds thoroughly precocious! Joan Gale Thomas illustrated.

Mr Pink-Whistle *(4 books, the first in 1941, and short stories)*

He is a busy little man who hates anything unfair or unkind and goes about righting wrongs - a sort of Enid Blyton 'Batman'! His cat Sooty takes the part of the ever-faithful 'Robin'. Dorothy Wheeler is in her element with superb illustrations.

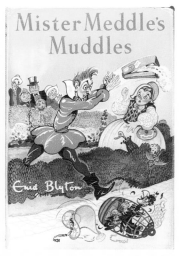

Far Left: Newnes, 1940.

Left: Newnes, 1950.

Both illustrated by Joyce Mercer and Rosalind Turvey.

Right: Newnes, 1941.

Far Right: Newnes, 1951.

Both illustrated by Dorothy Wheeler.

Far Left: Methuen, 1940. Illustrated by Joan Gale Thomas.

Left: Sunny Stories No.224, April 1941. Cover illustration by Joan Gale Thomas.

Right : Newnes, 1941.

Far Right: Newnes, 1955.

Both illustrated by Dorothy Wheeler.

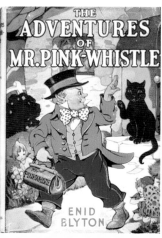

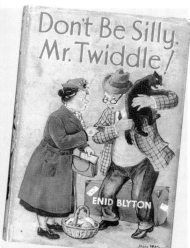

Right: Newnes, 1942.

Far Right: Newnes, 1949.

Both illustrated by Hilda McGavin.

All published by Brockhampton in 1942, 1944, 1947 and 1956. Illustrated by Olive Openshaw except the cover illustration on the 1956 edition which is by Fred White.

Above: Newnes, c.1946. Illustrated by Dorothy Wheeler.

Left: Evans, 1945. Illustrated by Gwen White.

Mr Twiddle *(3 books, the first in 1942, and many short stories)*

The bespectacled Mr Twiddle suffers many a misfortune due to his absent-mindedness, to the continual dismay and annoyance of his nagging wife. He started life in *Teachers World* as Mr Widdle, but after appearing in 'Mr Widdle on the Train', somebody must have had a discreet word with Enid because he gained a 'T' in his next appearance! Hilda McGavin illustrated.

Mary Mouse *(26 books, the first in 1942)*

Mary Mouse has a passion for cleaning. She leaves her family, who live in a 'hole', to take up residence with the Doll family. She becomes a right little Mary Poppins, keeping the Doll's house spotless and at the same time tending to all the needs of the three children, Melia, Pip and Roundy. The 23 picture strip books were initially made from *Picture Post* cut-offs during the war. Mary Mouse enjoyed longevity, appearing before the Famous Five and having her final adventure after them in 1964. Olive Openshaw did the early illustrating, while Fred White took over in the mid 1950s.

John Jolly *(4 books, the first in 1942)*

John Jolly was a small boy in a series of wartime stripbooks illustrated by Gwen White. Apparently the series didn't sell well as the intended six books were reduced to four and there were no reprints. They are now rare items eagerly sought by collectors.

Dame Slap *(1 book, first published in 1943)*

Dame Slap is another picture strip character illustrated by Dorothy Wheeler. The Dame is not to be confused with the ferocious schoolmistress of the same name in The Faraway Tree series. Okay, so both are schoolmistresses, but whereas the former is a tall elderly woman in need of a sense of humour transplant, this one is a big, comfortable rabbit much loved by her young charges.

The Three Golliwogs *(1 book, first published in 1944 and many short stories)*

These 'lovable toys', who live in a pretty little cottage with yellow walls and a blue gate with honeysuckle over the door, feature in a number of short stories illustrated by Joyce Johnson.

Pip *(2 books, the first in 1948, and short stories)*

Pip the Pixie was the first Enid Blyton character to appear in book form from a publication other than *Teachers World* or *Sunny Stories*. His adventures, which revolve round the birds, animals and insects of the countryside, originally appeared each week in the *Sunday Graphic* during the 1940s. Sixty of these stories are gathered in two books illustrated by Raymond Sheppard.

The Twins *(6 books, the first in 1948)*

Although Enid wrote short stories about several sets of twins, Johnny and Jinny were the only ones to feature in a number of books; six in all, the first in the Brockhampton Nursery Series and the other five as part of their Little Book Series. Eileen Soper illustrated them all.

Bumpy *(1 book, first published in 1949)*

Yet another character from a *Sunny Stories'* picture strip illustrated by Dorothy Wheeler. Bumpy is a funny little fellow who owns a hot-tempered bus, and three children, Anne, Michael and Biddy travel in it to a number of magical places.

Mr Tumpy *(4 books, the first in 1949 and short stories)*

Mr Tumpy owns a caravan that walks on its own bare feet. He, his friend, Spells and his dog, Bits, share a number of picture strip adventures. These first appeared daily in the *Evening Standard* during the 1940s. The drawings are another Dorothy Wheeler masterpiece.

Rubbalong *(2 books, the first in 1949 and short stories)*

Also in the *Evening Standard* were the stories about little Rubbalong and his Ma, who is a bit of a whizz with spells, which makes life awkward for 'nasties' - such as Grabbit and his sister, Mrs Well-I-Never. Twenty-two of the stories were collected into a book illustrated by Norman Meredith, who also illustrated a cut-out 'show' book.

Tiny *(1 book, first published in 1949 and short stories)*

Tiny is a five year old girl who appeared in a number of 'tiny' stories on Enid Blyton's monthly page in *Good Housekeeping* during the 1940s. Thirty-one of these stories have been gathered into one-pagers in a book illustrated by Eileen Soper.

Mandy, Mops and Cubby *(4 books, the first in 1952 and short stories)*

They are respectively a doll, a golly and a mouse, who set up house together in the garden of Mary Quite Contrary. Apart from four strip books they appeared in several annuals during the 1950s all drawn by Dorothy Wheeler.

Gobo *(2 books, the first in 1953)*

Mr Gobo lives in a little spinning house. He is half-goblin and half-brownie and is nearly always smiling. There were only two strip books here with an uncredited illustrator so perhaps the young readers didn't smile.

Clicky *(9 books, the first in 1953)*

Clicky is a clockwork clown who, like Noddy, was carved out of wood, but whereas Noddy needs Big-Ears to wind him up, Clicky needs a key. He is a bit of a square peg in a round hole, until he finds his niche in a circus. Eight strip books and a painting book is the total Clicky output all drawn by Molly Brett.

Bom *(14 books, the first in 1956, and short stories)*

Bom, the little toy drummer and his companion Wuffy Dog were popular in the mid to late 1950s, with a number of books appearing and a regular weekly spot in the *TV Comic*. R.Paul-Höye illustrated everything in the Bom line.

Rumble and Chuff *(2 books, the first in 1958, and short stories)*

They started life on a children's page in *Wife and Home* in 1953, but weren't put into books until the late 1950s. The stories about a quaint little engine and its driver were perhaps Enid's equivalent of Thomas the Tank Engine!

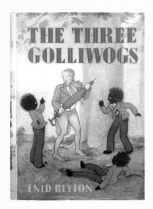

Newnes, 1944. Illustrated by Joyce Johnson.

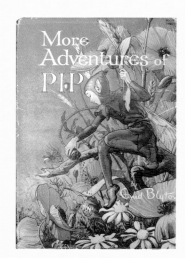

Sampson Low, 1948. Illustrated by Raymond Sheppard.

Brockhampton, 1948. Illustrated by Eileen Soper.

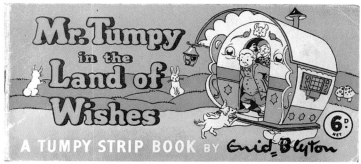

Sampson Low, 1953. Illustrated by Dorothy Wheeler.

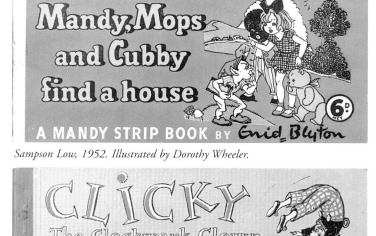

Sampson Low, 1952. Illustrated by Dorothy Wheeler.

Sampson Low, 1955. Illustrator unknown.

Brockhampton, 1953. Illustrated by Molly Brett.

Newnes, 1949. Illustrated by Dorothy Wheeler.

Brockhampton, 1956. Illustrated by R. Paul-Höye.

Macmillan, 1949. Illustrated by Norman Meredith.

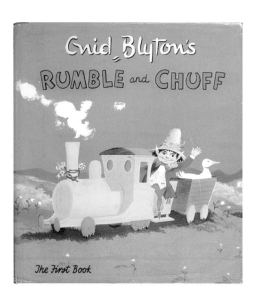

Littlebury, 1949. Illustrated by Eileen Soper.

Juvenile Productions, 1958. Illustrated by David Walsh.

Brockhampton, 1960. Illustrated by R. Paul-Höye.

ENID BLYTON'S Noddy is one of the most recognisable icons in British culture. Noddy books of all shapes and sizes have been produced - strip, tall, giant, tiny, pop-up, big and board - all took their place alongside the regular Noddy Library. In roughly a twenty year period between his conception and Enid's death, 154 books of various shapes and sizes graced the shelves of the bookshops. When a child wasn't actually reading it was possible to pass the time from breakfast to bed with a mountain of merchandise. Even when sleeping our child could still be in Noddy nightdress or pyjamas, tucked in with Noddy sheets beside a Noddy bedside light, which if turned on would reveal both Noddy wallpaper and curtains.

Noddy began when David White, the Managing Director of Sampson Low, Marston and Company Ltd, was keen to begin a new series of books with Enid Blyton. He wanted her to create a popular character for younger children with bright and colourful illustrations.

David met Enid at his Mayfair office, and showed her sample work by a number of illustrators.

Enid selected the Dutch artist Eelco Martinus ten Harmsen van der Beek (1897-1953), who had provided a few illustrations for her book *The Fourth Holiday Book*, published in July 1949. She insisted on meeting the artist before considering ideas for the new series. Beek travelled over from Amsterdam for the arranged meeting with Enid and within two hours they had imagined *Noddy Goes To Toyland* through words and

*Illustration by Beek in Enid Blyton's **The Fourth Holiday Book**, published by Sampson Low in 1949. Beek is listed as Eelco M.T.H. Van der Beek and the book was published in July, four months before the first Noddy book.*

sketches. A collaboration was enthusiastically agreed, with Enid and van der Beek each receiving a 5 per cent royalty. Enid usually got 15 per cent, but accepted a lower rate because the books were going to be heavily illustrated in colour. Within four days Enid had sent off the first two Noddy books to David White with the accompanying note:

'I have finished the first two Little Noddy Books, and here they are. I have written them with a view to give Van Beek all the scope possible for his particular genius - toys, pixies, goblins, Toyland, brick-houses, dolls houses, toadstool houses, market- places - he'll really enjoy himself! I don't want to tell him how to interpret anything because he'll do it much better if he has a perfectly free hand - but as Noddy (the little nodding man), Big-Ears the Pixie, and Mr and Mrs Tubby (the teddy bears) will probably feature in further books, and will be 'important' characters as far as these books are concerned, I'd be very glad if he could sketch out these characters and let me see roughs'.

Beek worked quickly and soon Enid had received the first of many beautiful illustrations. Both daughters remember their mother unpacking the artwork with great excitement and delight. Enid lay them out in the lounge. Van der

Beek, she said, had created Noddy and his environment exactly as she had visualised them.

The first book, *Noddy Goes To Toyland*, was published in the autumn of 1949 and was immediately popular, considerably exceeding expected sales. Further books followed, and Enid was contracted to write a Noddy strip for the *Evening Standard.*

Noddy toys and games soon followed. In the early days Beek illustrated everything to do with Noddy, but the work soon overwhelmed him, his health deteriorated and Sampson Low set up a stable of artists to help him. Most prominent among these was

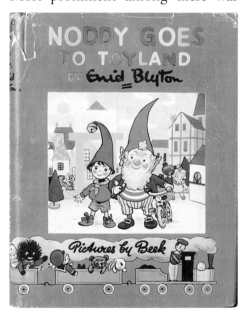

*The first Noddy book - **Noddy Goes to Toyland**, published by Sampson Low in 1949 and illustrated by Harmsen van der Beek. It was Enid's idea to use the Toyland train full of characters running round the covers to give the book a 'series' look.*

the talented Robert Tyndall, who was given clear and detailed instructions by van der Beek on how Noddy and the Toyland characters should be represented. When Beek died in 1953, Robert Tyndall was able to ensure a continuity of style.

Robert Tyndall seen here with some of his own sketches at the 1998 Enid Blyton Day.

Photo: Doreen James.

He sent his artwork to Enid for approval, and apart from once commenting that he had allowed Noddy's hair to grow too long, she was always generous with her praise for his work.

In 1954 Enid decided, with the encouragement of her agent George Greenfield, to write a Noddy pantomime. It took her just two weeks and the script was passed to the producer Bertie

*Music Sheet from the play, **Noddy in Toyland** published by Ricordi in 1954.*

Meyer, who quickly employed André van Gyseghen as director, and Philip Green as composer

for the music. Robert Tyndall designed the sets. Bookings were made for matinées over the Christmas period at the Stoll Theatre, which then had the largest seating capacity in London.

It sold out for every single performance during the pantomime season of 1954-5 and for the next six years enjoyed full houses at a variety of theatres.

From the theatre Noddy naturally progressed to television. Enid was very enthusiastic about her 'little nodding man' being chosen to feature in one of the first puppet series to be shown on the new British Commerical television channel. He made his television debut to popular acclaim in September 1955.

By Christmas 1958, over twenty million Noddy books had been sold in Britain and Australia, which included seventeen Noddy story books as well as eight big annuals and numerous little books. There were more than fifty licensees of Noddy merchandising in Great Britain selling hundreds of products. By 1962 over 26 million Noddy books had sold, and today the figure is well over 120 million copies.

*Artwork by Robert Tyndall for the dust jacket of **Noddy in Toyland, (Book of the Play)** published by Sampson Low in 1956. The text illustrations were by Wienk. Photo: Sotheby's.*

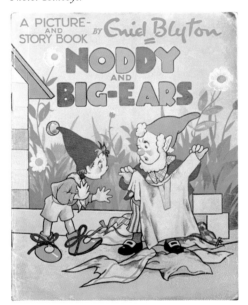

Sampson Low, 1952.
Illustrated by Harmsen van der Beek.

Trial for a pop-up book, early 1950s. It was never published !

Lawrence shows Noddy how to go faster, faster at Claxton Services on the M25. Parp! Parp!

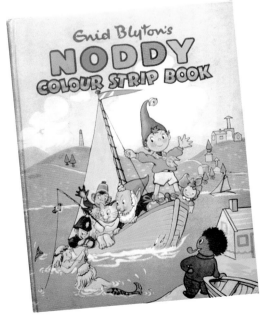

Sampson Low, 1952. Illustrated by Harmsen van der Beek.

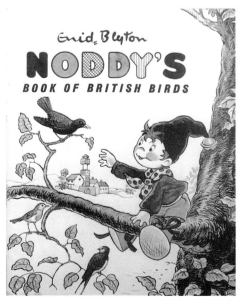

Chivers, 1958. Illustrated by Robert Tyndall.

"This is rather nice" said Noddy, picking up a blue doll's bonnet, **Noddy Goes to to Toyland, 1949.**   *Original Artwork by van der Beek. Photo: Sotheby's.*

'Noddy meets some silly hens' - **Noddy Storybook Treasury.**   BBC Children's Books, 1997.

Sampson Low, 1952.

Sampson Low, 1960. Illustrated by Robert Tyndall.

Noddy's name in French is Oui-Oui.   Sampson Low, 1952.   *Ricordi, 1950s.*
Illustrated by Harmsen van der Beek.

Packaging for Empire made Toys, 1959.

Noddy Quoits. Chad Valley, 1956.

Noddy Toilet Soap by Cullingford, 1978.

A clockwork Noddy produced by Louis Marx in the 1960s.

Character figures by Louis Marx, 1962.

Mr. Plod Egg Cup produced in the early 1960s.

Noddy Snakes and Ladders by Berwick, 1950s.

Noddy Letter Rack produced by Irene Series in 1963.

A Kellogg's Noddy Club Certificate, 1962.

"Noddy's Friends" Badge. Kellogg's, 1966.

Back of a packet of Kellogg's Ricicles, 1956.

Kellogg's Flick Book
Published in 1956.
Illustrated by Robert Tyndall.

Chivers Cake Tin, 1955.

Noddy Happy Families Card Game. Sampson Low, 1956.

Noddy Toothpaste
Cullingford, 1958.

Promotional Packaging for the Halex Noddy
Toothbrush, 1954.

Postcard published by
J. Salmon, 1954.

Noddy in Car by
Corgi, 1970.

Box and Board for the Little Noddy Car
Game by Bestime, early 1950s.

Bluebird, 1998

Walter Tuckwell in 1958. He was brought in to help with Noddy merchandising in the 1950s, because of his experience with Walt Disney. His stable later produced many talents, including a young whipper-snapper called Patrick Hawkey, later of Hawk Books.

Noddy Jigsaw Puzzle produced by Bestime, 1952.

Stories Retold

ENID enjoyed a good tale and particularly in the early part of her career she delighted in interpreting many a classic story in a manner that children could easily understand. She wrote extensively in *Teachers World* and *Sunny Stories* about Greek, Roman and Norse myths.

Latimer House, 1951. Illustrated by Anne and Janet Johnstone.

She also tackled weighty works such as *King Charlemagne and the Paladins of France, Stories of*

Latimer House, 1949. Illustrated by Joyce Johnson.

Chivalry in the Fourteenth Century, from Sir John Froissart's *Chronicles* and tales from Spencer's *Faerie Queene*.

Latimer House, 1950. Illustrated by Kathleen Gell.

Nearer to home she wrote a number of stories about both King Arthur and Robin Hood and even produced her own version of John Bunyan's *Pilgrim's Progress*, with the title *The Land of Far-Beyond*.

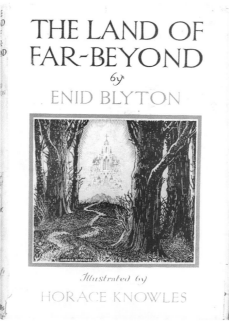

Published by Metheun, 1942. Illustrated by Horace Knowles. Enid's version of **The Pilgrim's Progress**.

Several classics got the Blyton treatment - Gulliver, Hiawatha, Aesop, the Brothers Grimm and Hans Christian Andersen all succumbed! Pantomimes such as Snow White, Cinderella, Puss in Boots, and Jack in the Beanstalk were all to play a part first in *Sunny Stories* and then in a series of film-strips that she directed herself.

Johnston & Bacon, 1955. Illustrated by Grace Lodge.

She was even quick off the mark to tell contemporary 'classics'. In 1941, just a short while after his first appearance she re-told six of Jean de Brunhoff's stories about Babar with illustrations redrawn from the original coloured volumes by Olive Openshaw, who a year later was to produce her first Mary Mouse illustrations.

Metheun, 1941. Illustrated by Olive Openshaw.

A. Wheaton, 1939. Text illustrations by Hugh Chesterman.

A. Wheaton, 1935.

Macmillan, 1950. Cover illustration by Jean Main. Text illustrations by Eileen Soper.

Johnston, 1939. Illustrated by Douglas Cuthill.

Enid wrote three major series of school readers and a number of lesser series as well. She also allowed her work to be included in a large number of school readers edited by other people, mostly in the 1930s and 1940s. Many of her readers inevitably contained recycled stories from various magazines, but the thirty books in the Pennant Series, published by Macmillan and once again illustrated by Eileen Soper, were all specially written and several contained strong moral messages with titles such as, 'Garry Give-Up and Fanny Find-a-Way'.

Johnston, 1937. Illustrated by Oxley.

Title page of Treasure Trove Reader Book 4, published by A. Wheaton in 1934. Illustrated by Hugh Chesterman.

Johnston & Bacon, 1955.

TELL-TALE TOMMY

Tommy was a tell-tale. Do you like tell-tales? No, you don't, and neither do I! So nobody liked Tommy very much, which was a pity, because he would have been quite a nice little boy if he hadn't been such a tell-tale.

16

'Tell-Tale Tommy' illustrated by Eileen Soper. A page from Pennant Reader No.14, published by Macmillan in 1950.

Bible Stories and Prayer Books

ENID BLYTON'S religious books have sold successfully the world over. Her gift for story telling and her ability to communicate through the written word was ideally suited for the task of re-telling bible stories for young children.

Methuen, 1943. Illustrated by Eileen Soper. The first book in which Enid re-interpreted the Bible for children.

It was in 1943 that Enid first used New Testament stories for a full-length book - *The Children's Life of Christ*. Published by Methuen it contained illustrations by Eileen Soper. The book's instant success ensured that many more religious books were to follow.

As a child Enid did not understand her baptism, held at Elm Road Baptist Church in 1910. It was the year her father left home, and a time of great suffering for her. Ironically, it was also the beginning of the period in which she was expected to lie to her closest friends and 'keep up appearances'. She was unable to gain comfort from religion, which both frightened and depressed her, and it appears that the God that she was

Methuen, 1944. Illustrated by Eileen Soper.

taught about was a threatening and angry masculine figure and she in turn had been made angry by this projection.

As an adult she did not belong to any particular church or denomination, nor did she regularly attend any form of church service. Sundays were, for her, a day to handle her accounts and answer correspondence.

Lutterworth Press, 1948. Illustrated by Elsie Walker. Gordon Hewitt wrote in the foreword to this book about the eight stories of Jesus, 'We asked her to write them because she is the best story-teller we know.'

In 1935 she was wrote to her friend Dorothy Richards:

'I do believe in God, though perhaps not your idea of God. I do trust him in that I believe that there is a real purpose and love behind everything and I do want to serve and love the highest - whatever and whoever that may be. I would like a personal God like yours, but I find it difficult to believe in one that you can talk to as you do.'

Enid did, however, make sure that both her daughters were baptised into the Anglican faith, were taught prayers and attended the local Sunday School.

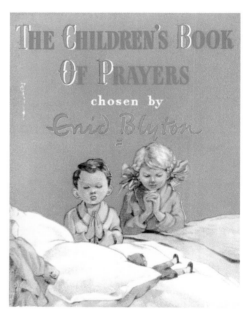

Frederick Muller, 1953. Illustrated by Grace Lodge.

She was extremely adept at interpreting the bible and was able to capture children's interest and imaginations. In her books Enid was able to project a clear and simple morality. Her religious books were apparently 'backed by ministers of all creeds' and were very highly regarded indeed.

BEFORE I GO TO SLEEP

Illustrated by GRACE LODGE

by Enid Blyton

Before I Go To Sleep *- a book of Bible stories and prayers for children at night - was published by Latimer House in 1947 and illustrated with period charm by Grace Lodge. The accumulated royalties, amounting to several thousand pounds, were donated by Enid to the children's convalescent home in Beaconsfield.*

THE GREATEST BOOK IN THE WORLD

Enid Blyton

British and Foreign Bible Society, 1954. Illustrated by Mabel Peacock.

Enid Blyton

A STORY BOOK OF JESUS

*Macmillan, 1956. Illustrated by Elsie Walker. With thirty-two glorious colour plates, the book cost eighteen shillings and sixpence. Of all Enid's books, only **The Teacher's Treasury** and **The Play's the Thing** cost more.*

Enid Blyton Bible Stories - Old and New Testaments. These were published by Macmillan in 1949 and 1953 respectively. There were twenty-eight readers and the two shown tell the tales of 'The Little Slave Girl', 'Daniel in the Lion's Den', 'The Boy who Left Home', and 'The Tale of The Good Samaritan'.

Brockhampton, 1947. Illustrated by Eileen Soper.

ENID wrote a number of books which were lavished with wonderful colour illustrations. Surprisingly the first of these came in the middle of the war when paper was at a premium.

Nor were they on the low quality paper common to many books of the period. Beautifully illustrated by Eileen Soper, they were printed on high quality shiny art paper. It was in fact only when paper ceased to be rationed in the early 1950s, that many of the picture books reverted to ordinary paper - presumably in an attempt to cut costs.

Brockhampton, 1947. Illustrated by Eileen Soper.

Brockhampton, 1949. Illustrated by Jeanne Farrar.

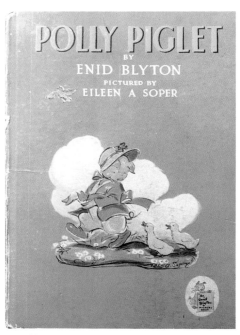

Brockhampton, 1943. Illustrated by Eileen Soper.

Brockhampton, 1949. Illustrated by Eileen Soper.

Brockhampton, 1950. Illustrated by Jeanne Farrar.

Illustration by Jeanne Farrar from
Oh! What a Lovely Time.
Brockhampton, 1949.

Brockhampton, 1951. Illustrated by Eileen Soper.

Birthday Time Book. Brent Press, c.1954.

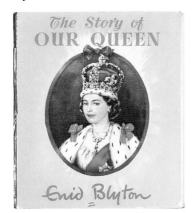

Frederick Muller,1953. Illustrated by F. Stocks May.

Waterlow, 1955. A book to help with adoption.

Collins, 1949. Photographs by Hugh Gee.

ENID wrote on a wide range of subjects. Birthdays and Christmas were both amply catered for; the Coronation was marked with *The Story of Our Queen*; or if you were a keen gardener, then Enid had a handy book for you.

Perhaps you preferred a visit to the zoo, in which case you were well prepared with what you might see there. You could even walk there as road safety was also covered in a colouring book with a story attached!

On a rainy day scissors could be used on a Werner Laurie Showbook or on the novelty book *Playing at Home*. There were also three books of photographs about Tinker the Kitten and two more about Belinda, a doll belonging to photographer Hugh Gee's daughter Jane, who also featured in the books.

If there was anything that children might be interested in, then Enid had the answer!

Latimer House, 1948. Illustrated by William McLaren

Pitkin, 1948. Illustrated by Connolly.

Advent Calendar. Hamish Hamilton, 1953. Illustrated by Fritz Wegner.

Pitkin, 1946. Illustrator unknown.

Methuen, 1955. Illustrated by Sabine Schweitzer.

Werner Laurie, 1950. Illustrated by Norman Meredith.

Newnes, 1943.
Illustrated by Ernest Aris.

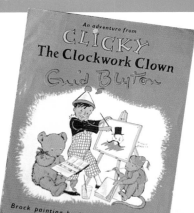
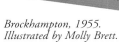

Brockhampton, 1955.
Illustrated by Molly Brett.

John Gifford, 1955. Cover by Hilda Boswell.

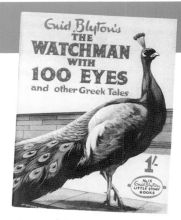

Johnston & Bacon, 1955.
Illustrated by Douglas Cuthill.

Original art by Harmsen van der Beek from **Noddy Goes to School**. Sampson, Low, Marston, 1952.

Harmsen van der Beek ranks alongside the greatest and most imaginative illustrators of the 20th century. He is the only illustrator for whom Enid specifically wrote for, devising characters with his style in mind.

Joseph Abbey	E. and R. Buhler
Lorna Adamson	Rene Bull
Marguerite Agopian	Doris Burton
G. Ambler	Alice Bush
Florence M. Anderson	W. Lindsay Cable
C. Andrews	R. Caille
I. Bennington Angrave	Susan Carruthers
Ernest Aris	Stavart J.Cash
G.W. Backhouse	Jenny Chapple
Kathleen Barnes	Phyllis Chase
Henry Barnett	Cedric Chater
Daphne V.Barry	Hugh Chesterman
Lewis Baumer	Lilian Chivers
Beattie	G.F. Christie
Beaurepaire	L.Church
Harmsen van der Beek	Arthur Clarke
Peter Beigel	Clem
John Bell	Rene Cloke
Molly Benatar	Frederick Cockerton
Alfred E. Bestall	Connolly
Binkie	A.Conolan
J. Blauwijkel	Anyon Cook
D.A. Boden	Jill Cooper
Hilda Boswell	Phyllis Cooper
George Bowe	Cyril Cowell
G.E.Breary	J.F. Cowell
Molly E. Brett	Hilda Cowham
L.R. Brightwell	Douglas Cuthill
H.M.Brock	Elsa Da Costa
Dorothy Brook	E.H. Davie
George Brook	Joyce Davies
E.Brooks	Marjorie L.Davies
Mary Brooks	L.Davy
Gail Brown	Ellen M. Dawson
Marda Brown	Phyllis Denton
R.Brown	Dickson
Lilian Buchanan	George S. Dixon

Christmas card, c.early 1920s.
Verse by Enid, Illustrated by Phyllis Chase.

Frontispiece by E.H.Davie to **Mr.Galliano's Circus**. Newnes, 1938.

Methuen, 1944. Illustrated by W.Lindsay Cable.

Johnston & Bacon, 1955.
Cover illustrated by Dickson.

Methuen, 1957.
Cover by Lilian Buchanan.

Johnston & Bacon, 1954.
Cover by John Dugan.

Collins, 1952.
Illustrated by Gilbert Dunlop.

Lutterworth Press, 1965.
Illustrated by Ruth Gervis.

John Dugan
Sheila Dungey
Gilbert Dunlop
Sheila Dunn
Jo Eaves
Mildred Entwisle
Treyer Evans
R.H.Evens
Ethel Everett
Jeanne Farrar
H.W. Felstead
Elizabeth Flinders
Marcia Lane Foster
G.Beuzeville Foyster
W.S.Foyster
Barbara C. Freeman
Jacques Fromont
William Fyffe
William J. Gale
Lucy Gee
Sally Gee
Kathleen M. Gell
Mary Gernat
Ruth Gervis
Iris Gillespie
Don and Ann Goring
E.M.Gorton
Roland Green
Dorothy Hall
H.J.Hardee
Pat Harrison
Ian Hassall
Rosemary Hay
Helen Haywood
Dorothy Heather
Racey Helps
T. Hewson
Geoffrey Higham

Francis E. Hiley
C. Holland
Cyril Holloway
G.M. Holt
Noel Hopking
Joyce Horn
Charlotte Hough
Joan Hoyle
Shirley Hughes
Leslie Illingworth
Beryl Irving
A.E. Jackson
Ena Jackson
Helen Jacobs
E.Jeffrey
Myrtle Jerrett
Joyce A. Johnson
Anne and Janet Johnstone
Grace Jones
Bruno Kay
Alfred Kerr
Tom Kerr
Denis G. King
May Kirkham
Horace J. Knowles
Betty Ladler
Lance
Jessie Land
Mary Kendal Lee
Robert Lee
Leo
J. Llewellyn
Stanley Lloyd
Grace Lodge
Kenneth Lovell
James Lucas
G.M. Luckraft
MacDowell

Sunny Stories No. 253,
November 1941.
Cover by Lucy Gee.

Brockhampton, 1948.
Illustrated by Kathleen Gell.

Brockhampton, 1959.
Illustrated by R. Paul-Höye.

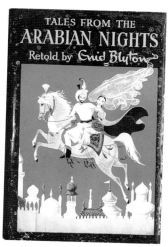

Above: Latimer House, 1951.
Illustrated by Anne & Janet Johnston

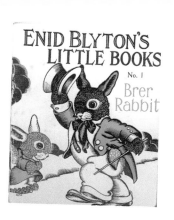

Far Left: Johnston & Bacon, 1960.
Illustrated by Grace Lodge.

Centre Left: Evans, 1942.
Illustrated by Alfred Kerr.

Left: *Sunny Stories for Little Folks,*
No.57, November 1928.
Cover by Joan Hoyle.
First cover with familiar red border.

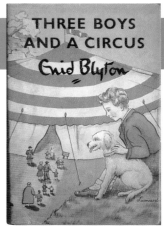

Newnes, 1945.
Illustrated by Kenneth Lovell.

Sunny Stories No.109, February 1939. Cover by Joyce Mercer.

Brockhampton, 1954. Illustrated by Olive Openshaw.

Werner Laurie, 1955. Cover by Leonardo.

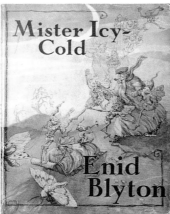

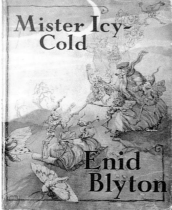

Newnes, 1953. Illustrated by Hilda McGavin.

Shakespeare Head Press, 1948. Illustrated by Will Nickless.

Sunny Stories for Little Folks No.27, August 1927. Cover by Dorothy Newsome.

Lutterworth Press, 1964. Illustrated by Daphne Rowles. Enid's last full legnth fictional work.

Robert MacGillivray
Hilda McGavin
William McLaren
Jean Main
Marion Main
E. Mansell
L.P.Marchant
Mary Martin
Winifred Martin
Mary N. Matthew
Helen May
Joan Martin May
F. Stocks May
A.L. Mazure
H.P. Meijer
Amy Joyce Mercer
Norman Meredith
Sally Michel
H.R. Millar
Tessa Mills
Janet E.Murray
Ruth Murrell
Donia Nachshen
W.E.Narroway
N.Newhouse
N.Newman
Newnham
Dorothy Newsome
Will Nickless
Kathleen Nixon
Nora
Richard B. Ogle
Galbraith O'Leary
Lola Onslow

Olive F. Openshaw
Doris Osborne
Oxley
Betty M.Page
Bip Pares
Frederick Parker
Cora E.M.Paterson
R. Paul-Höye
Roger Payne
Mabel Peacock
Tom Peddie
Yvonne Perrin
Rosa C. Petherick
N.Podgin
J.B.Prentice
Pierre Probst
S.W. Purvis
Benjamin Rabier
Anne Read
Christina Reed
Warwick Reynolds
Vera Rice-Jay
Agnes Richardson
Bernard Richardson
Jennifer M.Rickard
Eric Rickers
Philip Rickman
A.T. Riley
Lunt Roberts
Gordon Robinson
T.H. Robinson
Harry Rountree
Daphne B. Rowles
Norman R. Satchel

*Endpapers from **Rubbalong Tales**. Macmillan, 1949. Illustrated by Norman Meredith.*

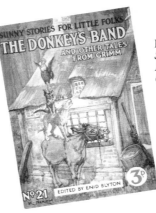

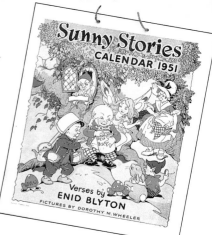

Left:
Sunny Stories for Little Folks No.21, May 1927. Cover by Kathleen Nixon.

Right:
Newnes, 1950. Illustrated by Dorothy Wheeler.

The Adventure of the SECRET NECKLACE
Enid Blyton

Lutterworth Press, 1954.
Illustrated by Isabel Veevers.

The VALLEY of ADVENTURE
Enid Blyton

Thames, 1960 (New edition).
Illustrated by Stuart Tresilian

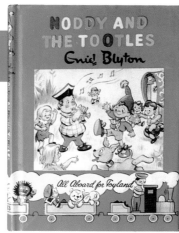

NODDY AND THE TOOTLES
Enid Blyton
All Aboard for Toyland.

Sampson Low, 1962.
Illustrated by Robert Tyndall.

Robert Tyndall was the 'visual creator' of Enid's popular character Bumpy dog, who made his first appearance in 1957.

Willy Schermelé
Sabine Schweitzer
Charles Seez
Caroline Sharpe
J. Sharpe
Burgess Sharrocks
Grace Shelton
Raymond Sheppard
M.G.Sherborne
Pat Simon
Romain Simon
Sinclair
R. Smethurst
Mary Smith
May Smith
Ben Somers
Eileen A.Soper
Vernon Soper
Joan Spearing
W. Spence
E. le M. Spilsbury
Spot
Cicely Steed
Ena Stell
Stevens
Stewart
Elizabeth Strickland
Susan
Valerie Sweet
Vander Syde
Eric Tansley
Vere Temple
Joan Gale Thomas
Eileen Thornley
Marjorie Thorp
Joan Thompson

Stuart Tresilian
Maurice Tulloch
John Turner
Rosalind M. Turvey
Robert Tyndall
Nora S. Unwin
S.Van Abbé
Frank Varty
Isabel Veevers
Sylvia I. Venus
Elsie Walker
Elizabeth Wall
David Walsh
John Wardle
K.M. Waterson
R. Webster
Fritz Wegner
R. Westcott
Dorothy M. Wheeler
Doris White
Frederick White
Gwen White
Jo White
Whyte
Wienk
Gladys Withers
Wilkin
R.James Williams
Violet M.Williams
Andrew Wilson
Edith Wilson
Robert Wilson
Gladys Withers
Woody

Rainy Day Stories
Enid Blyton

Rainy Day Stories
Enid Blyton

*The rough visual and the completed cover art for **Rainy Day Stories** published by Evans in 1952. Illustrations by Eileen Soper.*

Photo copyright Estate of George & Eileen Soper, controlled on behalf of the AGBI by Chris Beetles Ltd., London.

ADVENTURES OF THE WISHING-CHAIR
By ENID BLYTON

Newnes, 1953 edition.
Illustrated by Hilda McGavin.

Puzzle for the Secret Seven
Enid Blyton

Brockhampton, 1958.
Illustrated by Burgess Sharrocks.

MERRY MISTER MEDDLE!
Enid Blyton

Newnes, 1954. Illustrated by Joyce Mercer and Rosalind Turvey.

THE PUT-EM-RIGHTS
by ENID BLYTON

Lutterworth Press, 1946.
Illustrated by Elizabeth Wall.

1870

Enid's father, Thomas Carey Blyton born in Deptford, Kent.

1874

June 18 Enid's mother, Theresa Mary Harrison born in Sheffield.

1896

August 11 Thomas marries Theresa at St Peter's Church, Dulwich.

1897

August 11 Enid Mary Blyton born at 354 Lordship Lane, East Dulwich, the daughter of Thomas Carey Blyton, a cutlery salesman and Theresa (née Harrison).

Family move to a semi-detached villa at 95 Chaffinch Road, Beckenham.

October 8 Eelco Martinus ten Harmsen van der Beek born.

November Enid nearly dies from whooping cough, but is cradled all night in her father's arms.

1899

May 11 Enid's brother Hanly born.

1902

The family move to 35 Clock House Road, Beckenham.

Enid's brother Carey born.

1905

March 26 Eileen Alice Soper born.

1907

Enid starts at St Christopher's School for Girls, Beckenham.

About this time the family move a couple of doors down to another house at 31 Clock House Road, Beckenham.

1910

Shortly before her thirteenth birthday Enid's father leaves home for another woman.

Enid baptised at Elm Road Baptist Church.

1911

Enters Arthur Mee's children's poetry

Enid Blyton, aged 7.

13 Westfield Road, Beckenham.
Photo courtesy of Nicholas Reed.

St. Christopher's School lacrosse team. Enid is in the back row, second from right.

competition and is thrilled to get a letter from the writer, telling her that he intends to print her verses and would like to see more of her work.

1912

Enid and her family move to 14 Elm Road, Beckenham.

1913

Summer Enid travels to France with Mlle. Louise Bertraine, the French

teacher from her school St Christopher's. It is her first trip out of England.

1915

Enid's family move from Elm Road, Beckenham to a smaller semi-detached house nearby at 13 Westfield Road.

Enid leaves St Christopher's School. Moves into her friend Mary Attenborough's family home at 34 Oakwood Avenue, Beckenham.

34 Oakwood Avenue, Beckenham.
Enid lived here with the Attenboroughs between 1915 and 1919.

Bickley Park School,
Page Heath Lane, Bickley. Enid taught here in 1919.

Seckford Hall and Dovecote, near Woodbridge, Suffolk. The house had a secret passage that no doubt sparked off Enid's fertile imagination.

Ipswich High School, 1918. Enid can be seen standing in the centre of the top row.

1916

Attends the Guildhall School of Music.

Stays with George and Emily Hart at Seckford Hall, near Woodbridge, Suffolk. The hall with its 'haunted' bedroom, secret passage and surrounding farmland is a source of great delight and inspiration.

Enid decides to become a teacher after helping her friend Ida Hunt at Woodbridge Congregational Sunday School.

September Enrols on a National Froebel Union course at Ipswich.

She goes to Ipswich High School to train as a Kindergarten teacher and her contact with her family virtually ceases.

1917

March *Nash's Magazine* publish the first of three of her poems.

1918

December Qualifies as a teacher, completing her Froebel course.

1919

January Begins teaching at Bickley Park School, Bickley.

March Receives Teaching Certificate with Distinctions in Zoology and Principals of Education. 1st Class in Botany, Geography, Practice of Education, History of Education, Child Hygiene, Class Teaching and 2nd class in Literature and Elementary Mathematics.

1920

Moves to Southernhay, Hook Road, Surbiton to work as a nursery governess to the four children (David, Brian, Peter and John) of architect Horace Thompson and his wife Gertrude.

Renews acquaintance with her school friend, Phyllis Chase, who has begun to have some success as an illustrator. The two decide to submit work together, and it is to prove a turning point in their careers.

Enid's father, Thomas, dies unexpectedly of a heart attack at the age of fifty, while fishing on the Thames at Sunbury. Enid does not attend the Beckenham funeral.

1921

February 19 Wins a *Saturday Westminster Review* writing competition with 'On the Popular Fallacy that to the Pure All Things are Pure'.

More writing accepted by *The Londoner, The Bystander* and *Home Weekly.*

1922

February 15 Contributes first story 'Peronel and his Pot of Glue' to *Teachers World.* They also accept poems and other stories. She contributes to other journals and writes in annuals for both Cassell and Newnes.

June Her first book *Child Whispers* is published. Two stories published in books by Dean & Son, these are her first stories to appear in a book.

1923

Meets Major Hugh Alexander Pollock, an editor at the publishers George Newnes.

Earns more than £300 from her writing - equivalent to the price of a small suburban house.

March *Responsive Singing Games* published - her second book, and the only book for which she wrote the music.

July Gets her own column 'From My Window' in *Teachers World.* First article 'Genius and Childhood'.

1924

Enid is commissioned by Hugh Pollock to write a book on the zoo, and falls in love with him.

Above: **Nash's Magazine**, *March 1917.
Enid's first published poem was in this issue.
Right: A page from Enid's scrapbook
showing the poem.*

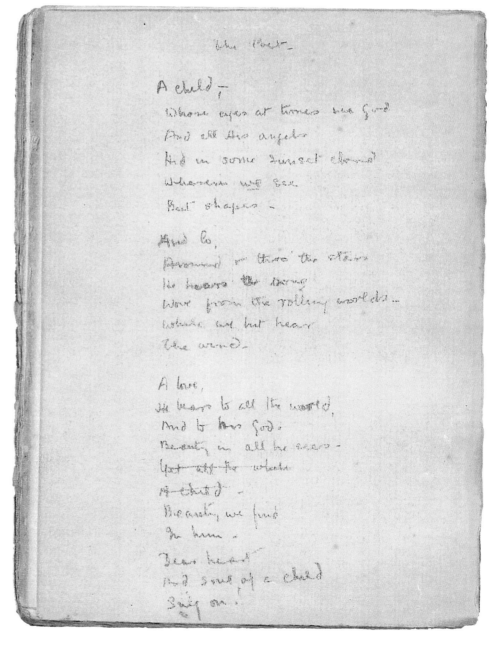

*Enid's rough draft for 'The Poet', later to be published in **The Poetry Review**, 1919. It was found in the back of one of Enid's own books, **The Poetry of Earth**, given to her as a present in March 1916.*

'Floppety Castle',
Enid's contribution to John Leng's
Fairyland Tales No.40, October 1922.

Sunny Stories for Little Folks No.3, August 1926.
Cover illustration by Ernest Aris.

Sunny Stories for Little Folks No.7, October 1926.
Cover illustration by Dorothy Newsome.

Enid Blyton on her wedding day,
August 28th, 1924.

One of Enid's typewriters.

Enid and Hugh spend a happy Easter at Seaford, Sussex with Mabel Attenborough, Mary's aunt.

July 3 Finishes *The Zoo Book* and joins Mabel for a holiday at Felpham.

August 28 Enid marries Major Hugh Alexander Pollock at Bromley Register Office. None of Enid's relations is invited to the wedding. Earns over £500 from writing.

They move into a top floor apartment at 32 Beaufort Mansions, Chelsea.

October *The Enid Blyton Book of Fairies* published - her first book of collected short stories.

1925

Annual earnings from writing reach £1095.10s.2d (equivalent to an executive's salary).

1926

February 26 Enid and Hugh move from Chelsea to their first 'real home' - Elfin Cottage, a newly built detached house in Shortlands Road (now number 83), Beckenham.

She purchases 'Bobs' a black and white smooth-haired fox-terrier.

July *Sunny Stories for Little Folks* first published, edited by Enid Blyton, who also writes everything.

October 1 *Teachers World* issue a special supplement containing a full-page interview with Enid Blyton. In the same issue Enid interviews A.A.Milne for an article. He presents her with an advance copy of his latest book - *Winnie the Pooh*.

November 10 - First appearance of Bobs for readers of 'From My Window'.

Teacher's Treasury (3 volumes) published - all written by Enid.

1927

Purchases her first typewriter and reluctantly learns how to use it.

Sunny Stories for Little Folks No.53, September 1928. Cover illustration by Ernest Aris.

Sunny Stories No.167, March 1940. Cover illustration by W. Lindsay Cable.

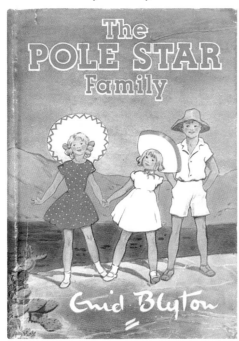

Lutterworth Press, 1950. Illustrated by Ruth Gervis. A cruise taken in 1930 gave Enid the inspiration for this story.

Also learns how to drive.

The Play's The Thing published. At 25/- it is to be the most expensive book in Enid's whole career.

August 31 First letter to the children in *Teachers World*.

1928

Enid consults a gynaecologist about her apparent infertility.

1929

August 2 Moves with Hugh to Old Thatch in Bourne End, Buckinghamshire. Starts asking children to collect silver paper and foil to raise money for Great Ormond Street, with great success.

August *Nature Lessons* published by Evans - the only book to contain her own illustrations.

September 4 Gets her own children's page in *Teachers World* - First letter from her dog, Bobs.

1930

October Enid and Hugh go on a cruise to Madeira and the Canary Islands aboard the *Stella Polaris*. This trip provides her with inspiration for *The Pole Star Family*, twenty years later.

1931

July 15 Enid's first daughter, Gillian Mary born - 8lbs 12oz in weight.

1932

February 5 - completes a full-length adult novel, *The Caravan Goes On*, but fails to find a publisher.

1933

Hugh works with Winston Churchill on the production of *The World Crisis*.

Gillian and her nurse sent to a residential nursery in London, while Enid and Hugh take a few weeks' holiday on their own in Scotland to help Hugh's health.

October *Letters from Bobs* published - written by Enid's pet fox-terrier. Within the first week ten thousand copies are sold.

December - Enid records in her diary Hugh's late homecomings.

1934

Hugh works with Churchill on editing *The Great War*.

Holiday at a small furnished house, Seaview, on the Isle of Wight.

Enid has a miscarriage.

April First four *Old Thatch Readers* published.

1935

October 27 Enid gives birth to Imogen Mary, 8lb 6 oz.

October 28 Dorothy Gertrude Richards, a nurse, comes to help Enid with Imogen.

November Enid's dog, Bobs, dies. He is buried in the garden, but Enid refuses to allow the gardener to mark his grave.

Dorothy leaves to take on another case, but the two remain close friends.

1936

Dorothy Richards accompanies Enid and her family on holiday to the Isle of Wight.

1937

January 15 *Sunny Stories* appears in new format, with long serial stories. The first of these is brought out in book form as *Adventures of the Wishing Chair* at the end of the year.

January 29 First Amelia Jane story in *Sunny Stories*.

1938

Spring Hugh suffers a serious bout of pneumonia. After a month in hospital he is discharged.

August 6 Enid, Hugh and their daughters move to a large house in Beaconsfield, Buckinghamshire. She asks readers to suggest a name - and 'Green Hedges' is chosen from the suggestions.

September *The Secret Island* published - the first of a series of 5 books.

September *Mr Galliano's Circus* published - the first of a series of 3 books.

December 30 First appearance of Mr Meddle in *Sunny Stories*.

1939

Outbreak of War. Printing paper is soon rationed. The initial quota is 50 per cent raised to 60 per cent in October.

May *The Enchanted Wood* published - the first in a series of 3 Faraway Tree books.

November *Boys' and Girls' Circus Book* published - Enid's first full-length unserialised book.

1940

Hugh rejoins his old regiment, The Royal Scots Fusiliers. Their marriage disintegrates.

May 3 First appearance of Mr Pink-Whistle in *Sunny Stories*.

Enid publishes 12 books including:

September *The Naughtiest Girl in the School* - the first in a series of 3 books and the first of Enid's school stories.

November First two books under the pseudonym of Mary Pollock published.

The Children of Cherry Tree Farm - the first full-length purpose written book that turns into a series.

Old Thatch is sold.

Newnes, 1934.
Cover illustration by Ian Hassall.
Interior illustrations by Kathleen Nixon.

The lawn and pond at Green Hedges.

1941

Sandy, the fox-terrier, disappears from Green Hedges. A teacher gives her a black and white short-haired terrier called Topsy, as a replacement. Enid meets surgeon, Kenneth Darrell Waters.

Publishes 8 books including:

May *The Adventurous Four* - the first in a series of 2 books.

November *The Twins at St Clare's* - the first in a series of 6 books.

Sunny Stories Calendar 1942 - her first calendar.

1942

Publishes 22 books including:

August *Enid Blyton's Readers 1-3* - the first use of her now famous logo-signature and the first work with Eileen Soper.

September *Five on a Treasure Island* - the first of a series of 21 books.

December Divorces Hugh.

Gillian sent to board at Godstowe Preparatory School, High Wycombe.

1943

October 20 Marries Kenneth Darrell Waters at the City of Westminster Register Office.

October 26 Hugh marries Ida at the City of London Register Office. Enid refuses Hugh permission to visit the children.

Publishes 23 books including:

December *The Mystery of the Burnt Cottage*, the first of the Find-Outers Mysteries - a series of 15 books

and *The Children's Life of Christ*, her first book re-telling tales from the Bible.

1944

Imogen sent to board at Godstowe Preparatory School, High Wycombe. Publishes 24 books in this year including:

November *The Island of Adventure* - the first of the Adventure series of 8 books.

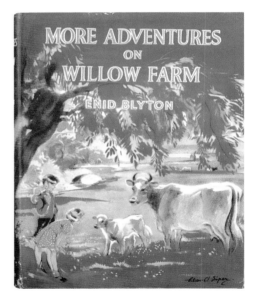

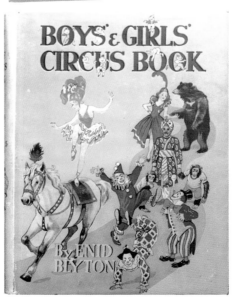

Above:
***Sunny Stories** Calendar 1942*
Newnes, 1941.
Illustrator unknown.

Centre Left:
***Sunny Stories** No.269, March 1942.*
Cover Illustration by Dorothy Wheeler.

Centre Right:
***Country Life**, 1943.*
Illustrated by Eileen Soper.

Newnes, 1942.
Illustrated by Hilda McGavin.

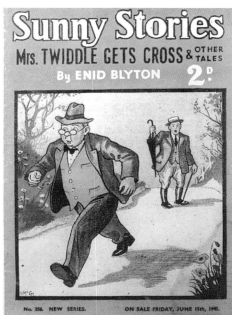

Sunny Stories No. 356, June 1945.
Cover illustration by Hilda McGavin.

Methuen, 1947.
Illustrated by Kathleen Gell.

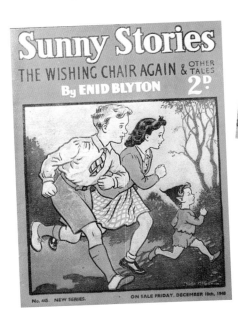

Sunny Stories No. 445, December 1948.
Cover illustration by Hilda McGavin.

Werner Laurie, 1948.
Illustrated by Eileen Soper.

Card Game by Pepys, 1950.
Illustrated by Dorothy Wheeler.

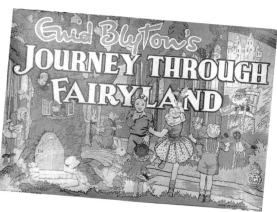

Board game by B.G.L. of Henley-on-Thames, late 1940s.
This was the first Blyton board game to be produced.

"To get a just estimate we left the judgement of Miss Blyton's work to a parliament of children.

The children loved her work and asked for more".

Yorkshire Post

Dorothy Richard's family bombed out of their home, and they move to Green Hedges. Enid asks them to leave after two days and Dorothy severs her friendship.

1945

Enid becomes pregnant, but miscarries after a fall.
End of War.
March Enid's first appearance in *Playways* - with 'The Caravan Family'.
November 14 Last 'Letter from Green Hedges' in *Teachers World*.

1946

July *First Term at Malory Towers* published - the first in a series of 6 books.
Doris Cox comes to work at Green Hedges as housemaid.

1947

September Imogen contracts polio.

1948

Travels on a trip to New York sailing out on the Queen Elizabeth and returning on the Queen Mary.
Imogen goes to Benenden.
October 6 Enid arrives in New York.
November publishes *Six Cousins at Mistletoe Farm* - the first of a series of 2 books.
Enid Blyton Diary published - her first diary.
First four Enid Blyton character jigsaws from Bestime.
'Journey Through Fairyland' by BGL - first Enid Blyton board game

1949

Publishers printing quotas no longer rationed.
Publishes 32 books including:
March *The Rockingdown Mystery* - the first in a series of 6 Barney Mysteries.

November *Noddy Goes to Toyland* - his first appearance.

November *The Secret Seven* - the first 'proper book' in a series of 15 books.

1950

March 31 Enid forms her own copyright holding company - Darrell Waters Limited

Other directors include Eric Rogers, Arnold Thirlby, Enid's solicitor, and John Basden, an accountant whose other clients include Sir Laurence Olivier and Ralph Richardson.

Enid gives over the royalties of *Before I Go to Sleep* to the Shaftesbury Society Babies' Home in Beaconsfield. It amounts to several thousand pounds.

Enid's mother dies.

'Faraway Tree' - first Enid Blyton card game from Pepys.

1951

Publishes 39 titles including *The Six Bad Boys* - in which she records some of the sadness she experienced when her father left home.

Enid and Kenneth purchase their own eighteen hole golf course at Studland Bay, Dorset.

Enid is nominated Queen Bee of the PDSA's Busy Bees' Club.

July 21 Enid's first appearance in *Mickey Mouse Weekly* with 'The Secret Seven'.

1952

Publishes 44 titles.

April Enid's first story in *The Busy Bees' News.*

September The Famous Five Club is formed.

September *The Story of My Life* published - Enid's autobiography for children.

1953

February 19 Enid withdraws from the magazine *Sunny Stories* after twenty-six years as editor.

March 18 First edition of *Enid Blyton's Magazine.*

Lutterworth Press, 1949.
Illustrated by Grace Lodge.

Pitkin, 1952.
Enid's autobiography.

Latimer House, 1949.
Illustrated by Grace Lodge.

Macmillan, 1949.
Illustrated by Stuart Tresilian.

Left to right: Gillian, Kenneth, Enid and Imogen at Green Hedges.

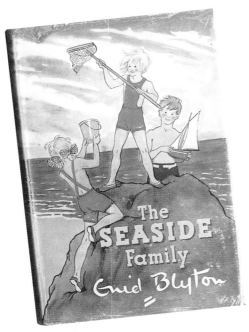

Lutterworth Press, 1950.
Illustrated by Ruth Gervis.

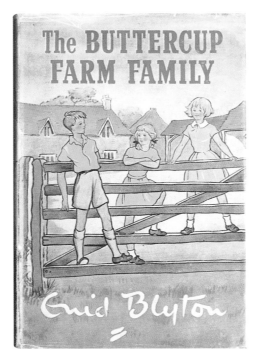

Lutterworth Press, 1951.
Illustrated by Ruth Gervis.

Macmillan, 1952.
Illustrated by Eileen Soper.

Evans, 1950.
Illustrated by Maurice Tulloch.

Newnes, 1950.
Illustrated by Dorothy Wheeler.

*Can you find the way to the ark? From the original artwork by Harmsen van der Beek for the **New Noddy Big Book** published by Sampson Low, Marston, 1954. This was one of the last illustrations Beek produced before his death in 1953.*

Photo: Sotheby's.

George Greenfield becomes Enid Blyton's agent.

July 24 Harmsen van der Beek dies.

1954

Enid renews her friendship with Dorothy Richards.

Enid becomes chairman of the committee for the Shaftesbury Society Babies' Home in Beaconsfield.

The pantomime *Noddy in Toyland* first performed. It takes Enid two weeks to write.

July 21 Enid Blyton's Magazine Club is formed.

December Enid resigns her directorship of Darrell Waters Ltd.

1955

Enid Blyton starts legal proceedings to quash rumours that she doesn't write her own books.

The Famous Five play produced for the Princes Theatre, London.

Kellogg's acquire the rights to use Noddy.

Noddy puppet films appear on Independent Television.

1956

Enid's first appearance in *TV Comic* with Noddy and Bom.

Buys Manor Farm at Stourton Caundle.

May Finishes adult play *Summer Storm*.

1957

Kenneth Darrell Waters retires as senior surgeon at St Stephen's Hospital, Fulham

Enid's health deteriorates.

Peter McKellar publishes *Imagination and Thinking*.

August Enid's daughter, Gillian, marries Donald Baverstock, a BBC producer at St James's Church, Piccadilly.

Five on a Treasure Island film serialised by the Children's Film Foundation for Saturday matinées.

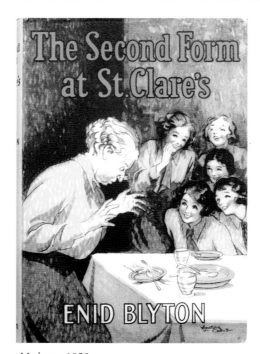

Methuen, 1953.
Illustrated by W. Lindsay Cable.

Johnston & Bacon, 1954.
Cover illustrated by Sinclair.

Weeties strip books given away with cereal in Australia in 1956.

Evans, 1955.
Illustrated by Grace Lodge.

The Busy Bees' News (P.D.S.A.), February 1957 issue.
Enid wrote in this as Queen Bee.

Five on a Treasure Island film, 1957.

1958
January Colin Welch publishes a vitriolic article criticising Noddy in *Encounter*

1959
September 9 Enid Blyton closes down *Enid Blyton's Magazine.*

1960
January 30 Enid's first appearance in *Princess* with 'Five at Finniston Farm'.

1961
October Hamlyn publish *The Big Enid Blyton Book*, the only book in which Enid broke her golden rule of never accepting a 'publisher's advance'.

1962
Gordon Landsborough launches Armada books so that children can buy their own paperback books. He sees Enid Blyton as the key to the success of the launch.
Noddy book sales reach 26 million copies.
Enid sells Manor Farm at Stourton Caundle, Dorset.

1963
May 25 Enid's first appearance in *School Friend* - with 'Bravo Secret Seven'.
July *Fun for the Secret Seven* the last in the series, published.

July *Five Are Together Again* published - the last in the series.

1964
February *Noddy and the Aeroplane* - the last book in the Noddy Library series.
Film *Five Have A Mystery To Solve* released by Rayant Pictures Ltd for the Children's Film Foundation.

1965
May *Mixed Bag* published - a song book for which her nephew, Carey Blyton writes the music.
August *The Man Who Stopped to Help* and *The Boy Who Came Back* published - the last full-length books to be written by Enid.

1967
Enid calls her brother, Hanly, after seventeen years without contact and begs him to visit.
September 15 Enid's husband, Kenneth, dies. She writes in her diary: 'My darling Kenneth died. I loved him so much. I feel lost and unhappy'.
Imogen marries Duncan Smallwood.

1968
November 28 Enid Blyton dies peacefully in her sleep in a Hampstead nursing home.

1969
January Memorial service held for Enid at St James's Church, Piccadilly.

1971
May 26 Green Hedges sold by auction.
November 6 Hugh Pollock dies.

1972
June 24 Enid appears in *Pixie* No.1 with 'The Naughtiest Girl In The School'.

1973
Green Hedges pulled down to make way for a housing development.

1974
March 9 *Noddy and His Friends* No.1 published by Hudvale.
April 29 *Story Teller Extraordinary* broadcast on BBC1 as part of 'The Success Story' series.
Barbara Stoney's *Enid Blyton - A Biography* first published.

1975
May 10 *Noddy Time* No.1 published by Womans Way.

1976
Enid's brother Carey dies.

1978
July 3 Famous Five Television series first shown, made by TVS.
July 22 Enid's first appearance in *Look In* No.30 with 'Five Have A Mystery To Solve'.

1982
In the Government's Survey of 10,000 eleven year olds Enid Blyton is voted the most popular author.
Sheila Ray publishes *The Blyton Phenomenon.*
Darrell Waters Ltd forms the Enid Blyton Trust for Children.
Film of *The Island of Adventure* broadcast on television made by Ebefilms Ltd.
October 20 *Rupert Weekly* first published - containing Noddy.
November 2 *Five Go Mad in Dorset* broadcast on Channel 4. A parody by the Comic Strip.

'Like wife-swapping in the Home Counties, the banning of Blyton seems to have been more a matter of rumour than of fact'.

Jeremy Lewis, 1982.

1983

Five Go Mad on Mescalin - the second parody made for television by the Comic Strip.

November Enid's brother, Hanly, dies.

1985

National Library for the Handicapped Child founded in memory of Enid Blyton by her daughter, Imogen.

September First issue of *Enid Blyton's Adventure Magazine.*

1988

April 3 *The Selling of Noddy* broadcast on ITV.

1989

Enid's daughter, Imogen, publishes *A Childhood at Green Hedges.*

1990

March 18 Eileen Soper died

May *The Enid Blyton Newsletter* started.

Film *The Castle of Adventure* broadcast on television made by TVS.

1991

Animated films based on St Clare's appear on Japanese Television.

The Sunday Times include Enid Blyton in the 1000 Makers of the 20th Century.

1992

January Michael Rouse publishes *Green Hedges Magazine.*

March Richard Walker forms Blyton Book Collectors' Society.

October 14 BBC publish first issue of *Noddy Magazine.*

December 26 *Sunny Stories* broadcast on BBC 2 made by the Bookmark programme.

Fabbri publish *Five on a Treasure Island* as No.50 in their Classic Adventure series.

1993

March 6 First Enid Blyton Day held at Rickmansworth.

1995

February Trocadero plc acquire Darrell Waters Ltd at £14.6 million and change the name to Enid Blyton Ltd.

Enid Blyton Society formed.

'Adventure Series' (8 films) filmed in New Zealand by Cloud 9/CLT.

September 10 New Famous Five Television series first screened on ITV made by Zenith North.

1996

July Enid Blyton Society's first Journal.

October Centenary celebrations start with a reception at the Victoria and Albert Museum, London. An Enid Blyton award, called 'The Enid', is announced which is to be presented annually to the person judged to have contributed outstanding service to children.

October The first Noddy CD Rom released by the BBC.

December Enid's signature included in the Regent Street illuminations with Noddy leading the parade for the switching-on ceremony.

December 16 *Secret Lives* - a TV documentary on Enid Blyton broadcast on Channel 4.

'Secret Series' (5 films) filmed in New Zealand by Cloud 9/CLT.

1997

January *The Famous Five* Musical opens and tours for six months, produced by King's Head Theatre.

March 26 First issue of *Enid Blyton's Mystery and Suspense Magazine.*

April 6 Model of Green Hedges unveiled at Bekonscot by Gillian Baverstock.

April 12 Enid Blyton: A Celebration and Reappraisal - a conference held by the National Centre for research in Children's Literature at Roehampton Institute. The papers, edited by Nicholas Tucker and Kimberley Reynolds, are published later in the year.

June Tony Summerfield publishes *Enid Blyton A Comprehensive Bibliography.*

Gillian Baverstock publishes *Enid Blyton* (Tell Me About Writers Series).

June David Rudd gets a Phd on the subject of Enid Blyton and the Mystery of Children's Literature (Sheffield Hallam University).

August 11 English Heritage plaque on Southernhay unveiled by Gillian Baverstock.

September 9 Royal Mail Centenary stamps issued.

Centenary exhibitions held at the London Toy and Model Museum, Hereford and Worcester County Museum and Bromley Library.

Tom Adams completes his mixed media picture 'The Enid Blyton Lifescape'.

October 29 Noddy sale of original artwork held at Sotheby's, London. Harmsen van der Beek's illustrated letter to Enid fetches a hammer price of £35,000.

November 17 Blue Peter special on Enid Blyton.

1998

March 26 Enid Blyton's *Enchanted Lands* No.1 published by Redan.

May George Greenfield publishes his biography *Enid Blyton.*

August 30 The new 40 part series of Noddy makes its debut on American TV. The series also features real children and new puppet stars like Sherman the Tank Turtle and Gator Gerty.

November 21 *The Secret Seven Save the World* first performed at the Sherman Theatre, Cardiff.

November 24 *Noddy 2* sale held at Sotheby's, London.

December Johnny and Betty Hopton get a *Guinness Book of Records* Certificate for the largest Noddy collection in the world.

1999

Noddy's 50th. anniversary year.
The Enid Blyton Dossier published.

INTO THE FUTURE.........

Top Left: *3rd Edition, 1998.*
Top Right: *Noddy is appealing to a new generation. Oliver, 1999.*

Opening of model 'Green Hedges' at Bekonscot by Gillian Baverstock. April 6th, 1997.

The Enid Blyton Society

publishes three magazines a year and also holds a large annual meeting. For further information send a SAE to:-

The Enid Blyton Society
93 Milford Hill
Salisbury
Wiltshire
SP1 2QL

Into the future...The new marketing and brand strategies introduced by Enid Blyton Limited promise to bring the delights of her work to a new generation of children worldwide.

95

Select Bibliography

Gillian Baverstock, *Enid Blyton (Tell Me About Writers Series)*, 1997

Enid Blyton, *The Story of My Life*, 1952

Enid Blyton Society Journal, from 1996

Green Hedges Magazine, Numbers 1 - 24, 1992-1998

George Greenfield, *A Smattering of Monsters*, 1995

George Greenfield, *Enid Blyton*, 1998

Helen Macleod, 'Enid Blyton's Noddy', *Book and Magazine Collector* No.40, July 1987

Helen Macleod, 'Enid Blyton and her Famous Five Adventure Books', *Book and Magazine Collector* No.52, July 1988

Bob Mullan, *The Enid Blyton Story*, 1987

Sheila Ray, *The Blyton Phenomenon*, 1982

Nicholas Reed, *Enid Blyton in Beckenham and Bromley*, 1997, revised edition 1998

Eva Rice, *Who's Who in Enid Blyton*, 1997

David Rudd, *The Famous Five - A Character Guide*, 1995, revised edition 1997

Julia Sesemann, 'Enid Blyton', *Book and Magazine Collector*, No. 4, June 1984

Imogen Smallwood, *A Childhood at Green Hedges*, 1989

Barbara Stoney, *Enid Blyton - The Biography*, 1974, revised editions 1992 and 1997

Tony Summerfield, *A Comprehensive Bibliography of Enid Blyton*, 1997, revised edition 1998

Tony Summerfield, *Sunny Stories for Little Folks 1926-1936 - An Index*, 1998

Tony Summerfield & Norman Wright, *Enid Blyton's Sunny Stories 1937-1941 - An Index*, 1996

Tony Summerfield & Norman Wright, *Sunny Stories 1942-1953 - An Index*, 1995

Tony Summerfield & Norman Wright, *Enid Blyton's Magazine 1953-1959 - An Index*, 1994

Nicholas Tucker & Kimberley Reynolds (Edited by), *Enid Blyton: A Celebration & Reappraisal*, NCRL, 1997

Mason Willey, *Enid Blyton - A Bibliography of First Editions*, 1993

David Wootton, *The Art of George and Eileen Soper*, Chris Beetles Gallery, London, 1995

Norman Wright, 'Collecting Enid Blyton', *Books, Maps and Prints* Vol. 1 No.3, June 1989

Norman Wright, 'Enid Blyton Ephemera', *Book and Magazine Collector* No. 92, November 1991

Norman Wright, 'The World of Enid Blyton', *Antiquarian Book Monthly*, April 1994

Norman Wright, 'Enid Blyton - A Centenary Celebration', *Book and Magazine Collector* No.161, August 1997